DISNEYLAND'S HIDDEN MICKEYS

· ·

A Field Guide to

Disneyland®
Resort's

Best Kept Secrets

· · · · · · · · · · · · · · · · · · · ·

Fifth Edition

Steven M. Barrett

DISNEYLAND'S HIDDEN MICKEYS

A Field Guide to Disneyland® Resort's
Best Kept Secrets
5th edition

Published by
The Intrepid Traveler
P.O. Box 531
Branford, CT 06405
http://intrepidtraveler.com

Copyright ©2015 by Steven M. Barrett
Fifth Edition
Printed in the U.S.A.
Cover design by Foster & Foster
Interior Design by Starving Artist Design Studio
Maps designed by Evora Taylor
Library of Congress Card Number: 2014946171
ISBN-13: 978-1-937011-48-2

10 9 8 7 6 5 4 3 2 1

Trademarks, Etc. • • • • • • • • •

This book makes reference to various Disney copyrighted characters, trademarks, marks and registered marks owned by The Walt Disney Company and Disney Enterprises, Inc.

All references to these properties, and to The Twilight Zone®, a registered trademark of CBS, Inc., are made solely for editorial purposes. Neither the author nor the publisher makes any commercial claim to their use, and neither is affiliated with either The Walt Disney Company or CBS, Inc. in any way.

Also by Steven M. Barrett

Hidden Mickeys:
A Field Guide to Walt Disney World's
Best Kept Secrets

Hidden Mickeys Go To Sea:
A Field Guide to the Disney Cruise Line's
Best Kept Secrets

Dedication . . . .

I dedicate this book to my wife Vickie and our son Steven, who support and help me with my Hidden Mickey passion, and to the many wonderful Hidden Mickey fans I've met through my website and in the Disney parks.

Photo by Vickie Barrett

About the Author ● ● ● ● ● ● ● ● ●

Author Steven M. Barrett paid his first visit to Disneyland as a child. He has hunted Hidden Mickeys at Disneyland for years and wrote his first *Disneyland's Hidden Mickeys* book in 2007. Because new Hidden Mickeys appear over time and others are lost, he updates the book every few years. In this book, you'll find a Hidden Mickey Scavenger Hunt for each of the theme parks, along with a third hunt that includes Downtown Disney District, the three resort hotels, and other areas on Disneyland property. To organize the Scavenger Hunts for efficient touring, Steve consulted various guidebooks and conducted his own research.

Notes

True to their name, Hidden Mickeys are elusive. New ones appear from time to time and some old ones disappear (see page 15, paragraph 3). When that happens—and it will—I will let you know on my website:

www.HiddenMickeyGuy.com

So if you can't find a Mickey—or if you're looking for just a few more—be sure to check it out.

***

Thank You, My Fellow
Hidden Mickey Hunters

No Hidden Mickey hunter works alone. Scores of dedicated Mickey sleuths have helped me find the elusive Mouse. Thanks to each and every one of you. You'll find your names in the Acknowledgements, beginning on page 139.

Table of Contents

Read This First! • • • • • • • • • • •

My guess is that you have visited Disneyland before, perhaps many times. But if I've guessed wrong, and this is your first visit, then this note is for you.

Searching for Hidden Mickeys is lots of fun. But it's not a substitute for letting the magic of Disney sweep over you as you experience the Disneyland parks for the first time. For one thing, the scavenger hunts I present in this book do not include all the attractions in the Disneyland theme parks. That's because some of them don't have Hidden Mickeys! For another, the first-time visitor should get ready for fun by also consulting a general Disneyland Resort guidebook for descriptions of Disneyland attractions, shows, dining, and other tourist information.

That doesn't mean you can't search for Hidden Mickeys, too. Just follow the suggestions in Chapter One of this book for "Finding Hidden Mickeys Without Scavenger Hunting."

CHAPTER 1

Hidden Mickey Mania

Have you ever marveled at a "Hidden Mickey"? People in the know often shout with glee when they recognize one. Some folks are so involved with discovering them that Hidden Mickeys can be visualized where none actually exist. These outbreaks of Hidden Mickey mania are confusing to the unenlightened. So let's get enlightened!

Here's the definition of an official Hidden Mickey: a partial or complete image of Mickey Mouse that has been hidden by Disney's Imagineers and artists in the designs of Disney attractions, hotels, restaurants, and other areas. These images are designed to blend into their surroundings. Sharp-eyed visitors have the fun of finding them.

The practice probably started as an inside joke among the Imagineers (the designers and builders of Disney attractions). According to Disney guru Jim Hill (JimHillMedia.com), Hidden Mickeys originated in the late 1970s or early 1980s, when Disney was building Epcot and management wanted to restrict Disney characters like Mickey and Minnie to Walt Disney World's Magic Kingdom. The Imagineers designing Epcot couldn't resist slipping Mickeys into the new park, and thus "Hidden Mickeys" were born. Guests and "Cast Members" (Disney employees) started spotting them and the concept took on a life of its own. Today, Hidden Mickeys are anticipated in any new Disney construction anywhere, and Hidden Mickey fans can't wait to find them.

Hidden Mickeys come in all sizes and many forms. The most common is an outline of Mickey's head formed by three intersecting circles, one for Mickey's round head and two for his round ears. Among Hidden Mickey fans, this image is known as the "classic" Hidden Mickey, a term I will adopt in this book. Other Hidden Mickeys include a side or oblique (usually three-quarter)

profile of Mickey's face and head, a side profile of his entire body, a full-length silhouette of his body seen from the front, a detailed picture of his face or body, or a three-dimensional Mickey Mouse. Sometimes just his gloves, handprints, shoes, or ears appear. Even his name or initials in unusual places may qualify as a Hidden Mickey.

And it's not just Mickeys that are hidden. The term "Hidden Mickey" also applies to hidden images of other popular characters. There are Hidden Minnies, Hidden Donald Ducks, Hidden Goofys, and other Hidden Characters in the Disneyland Resort, and I include many of them in this book.

The sport of finding Hidden Mickeys is catching on and adds even more interest to an already fun-filled Disneyland vacation. This book is your "field guide" to more than 480 Hidden Mickeys in the Disneyland Resort. To add to the fun, instead of just describing them, I've organized them into three scavenger hunts, one for each of the theme parks and one for all the rest of the Disneyland Resort: Downtown Disney District, the resort hotels, and beyond. The hunts are designed for maximum efficiency so that you can spend your time looking for Mickey rather than cooling your heels in lines. Follow the Clues and you will find the best Hidden Mickeys Disneyland has to offer. If you have trouble spotting a particular Hidden Mickey (some are extraordinarily well-camouflaged!) you can turn to the Hints at the end of each scavenger hunt for a fuller description.

Scavenger Hunting for Hidden Mickeys

To have the most fun and find the most Mickeys, follow these tips:

★ **Arrive early** for the theme park hunts—45 minutes ahead of your entry time. If you're eligible for early entry (because you're holding a special ticket

that allows early entry or you are staying in one of the three Disney Hotels and hold any valid park admission ticket), arrive at the early-entry park for that day 45 minutes or so before the early entry opening time. If you're not eligible for early entry, go to the non-early entry park for that day and arrive 45 minutes before the official opening time.

Pick up a Guidemap and Times Guide and plot your course. Then look for Hidden Mickeys in the waiting area while you wait for the rope to drop. You'll find the Clues for those areas by checking the Index to Mickey's Hiding Places in the back of this book. Look under "Entrance areas." You'll notice that headliner attractions are the first stops in the scavenger hunts. If you arrive later in the day, you may want to pick up a FASTPASS for the first major attraction and then skip down a few Clues to stay ahead of the crowd.

★ "Clues" and "Hints"
Clues under each attraction will guide you to the Hidden Mickey(s). If you have trouble spotting them, you can turn to the Hints at the end of the hunt for a fuller description. The Clues and Hints are numbered consecutively, that is, Hint 1 goes with Clue 1, so it's easy to find the right Hint if you need it. In some cases, *Soarin' Over California* in Disney California Adventure for example, you may have to ride the attraction more than once to find all the Hidden Mickeys.

★ Scoring
All Hidden Mickeys are fun to find, but all Hidden Mickeys aren't the same. Some are easier to find than others. I assign point values to Hidden Mickeys, identifying them as easy to spot (a value of 1 point) to difficult to find the first time (5 points). I also consider the complexity and uniqueness of the image: the more complex or unique the Hidden Mickey, the higher the point value. For example, some of the easy-to-spot Hidden Mickeys in Mickey's Toontown in Disneyland are one- or two-point Mickeys. The brilliantly camouflaged Mickey hiding in the tree on one of the ceramic panels decorating a column outside Disney's Grand Californian Hotel & Spa is a five-pointer.

★ Playing the game
You can hunt solo or with others, competitively or just for fun. There's room to tally

your score in the guide. Families with young children may want to focus on one- and two-point Mickeys that the little ones will have no trouble spotting. (Of course, little ones tend to be sharp-eyed, so they may spot familiar shapes before you do in some of the more complex patterns.) Or you may want to split your party into teams and see who can rack up the most points (in which case, you'll probably want to have a copy of this guide for each team).

Of course, you don't have to play the game at all. You can simply look for Hidden Mickeys in attractions as you come to them. (See "Finding Hidden Mickeys Without Scavenger Hunting" below.)

★ Following the Clues
The hunts often call for crisscrossing the parks. This may seem illogical at first, but trust me, it will keep you ahead of the crowd. Besides, it adds to the fun of the hunt and, if you're playing competitively, keeps everyone on their toes. Warning: Many Hidden Mickeys are waiting to be found in the Disney Parks. Depending on the crowds and the park hours when you visit, you may not be able to complete the Scavenger Hunt in one day!

★ Waiting in line
Don't waste time in lines. If the wait is longer than 15 minutes, get a FASTPASS (if available and you're eligible), move on to the next attraction, and come back at your FASTPASS time. Exception: In some attractions, the Hidden Mickey(s) can only be seen from the standby (regular) queue line, and not from the FASTPASS line. (I've not suggested FASTPASS in the Clues section when that is the case.) The lines at these attractions should not be too long if you start your scavenger hunt when the park opens and follow the hunt Clues as given. If you do encounter long lines, come back later during a parade or in the hour before the park closes. Alternatively, if you need to board an attraction with a long wait without a FASTPASS, use the Single Rider queue if available. (Check your Guidemap for a big "S" symbol next to the attraction.)

★ Playing fair
Be considerate of other guests. Some Hid-

den Mickeys are in restaurants and shops. Ask a Cast Member's permission before searching inside sit-down restaurants, and avoid the busy mealtime hours unless you are one of the diners. Tell the Cast Members and other guests who see you looking around what you're up to, so they can share in the fun.

Finding Hidden Mickeys Without Scavenger Hunting

If scavenger hunts don't appeal to you, you don't have to use them. You can find Hidden Mickeys in the specific rides and other attractions you visit by using the *Index to Mickey's Hiding Places* in the back of this book. For easy lookup, attractions are also listed under their appropriate "lands" (for example, Frontierland in Disneyland and Hollywood Land in Disney California Adventure). To find Hidden Mickeys in the attraction, restaurant, hotel, or shop you are visiting, turn to the *Index*, locate the appropriate page, and then follow the Clue(s) to find the Hidden Mickey(s).

Caution: You won't find every attraction, restaurant, hotel, or shop in the Index. Only those with confirmed Hidden Mickeys are included in this guide.

Hidden Mickeys: Real or Wishful Thinking?

The classic (three-circle) Mickeys are the most controversial, for good reason. Much debate surrounds the gathering of circular forms throughout Disneyland. The three cannonball craters in the wall of the fort in *Pirates of the Caribbean* (Clue 35 in the Disneyland Park Scavenger Hunt) is obviously the work of a clever artist. However, three-circle configurations occur spontaneously in art and nature, as in collections of grapes, tomatoes, pumpkins, bubbles, oranges, cannonballs, and the like. Unlike the cannonball crater Hidden Mickey in *Pirates of the Caribbean*, it may be difficult to attribute a random "classic Mickey" configuration of circles to a deliberate Imagineer design.

So which groupings of three circles qualify as Hidden Mickeys as opposed to wishful thinking? Unfortunately, no master list of actual or "Imagineer-approved" Hidden Mickeys exists. Purists demand that a true classic Hidden Mickey should have proper proportions and positioning. The round head must be larger than the ear circles (so that three equal circles in the proper alignment would not qualify as a Hidden Mickey). The head and ears must be touching and in perfect position for Mickey's head and ears.

On the other hand, Disney's recent mantra is: "If the guest thinks it's a Hidden Mickey, then by golly it is one!" Of course, I appreciate Disney's respect for their guests' opinions. However, when the subject is Hidden Mickeys, let's apply some guidelines. My own criteria are looser than the purist's but stricter than the "anything goes" Disney approach. I prefer to use a few sensible guidelines.

To be classified as a genuine classic Hidden Mickey, the three circles should satisfy the following criteria:

1. Purposeful (sometimes you can sense that the circles were placed on purpose).

2. Proportionate sizes (head larger than the ears and somewhat proportionate to the ears).

3. Round or at least "roundish."

4. The ears don't touch each other, and the ears are above the head (not beside it).

5. The head and ears touch or they're close to touching.

6. The grouping of circles is exceptional or unique in appearance.

7. The circles are hidden or somewhat hidden and not obviously décor (decorative).

Having spelled out some ground rules, allow me now to bend them in one instance. Some Hidden Mickeys are sentimental favorites with Disney fans, even though they may actually represent "wishful thinking." (My neighbor, Lew Brooks, calls them "two-beer" Mickeys.) Who am I to defy tradition? For example, the three circles on the back of the turtle in *Snow White's Scary Adventures* (Clue 121 in the Disneyland Scavenger Hunt) form a not-quite-proportionate "classic" Mickey. However, if you ask Cast Members near this attraction about a Hidden Mickey, they may whisper to you these cryptic words: "Watch for the turtle!"

Hidden Mickeys vs. Decorative Mickeys

Some Mickeys are truly hidden, not visible to the tourist. They may be located behind the scenes, available only to Cast Members. You won't find them in this field guide, as I only include Hidden Mickeys that are accessible to the guest. Other Mickeys are decorative; they were placed in plain sight to enhance the décor. For example, in a restaurant, I consider a pat of butter shaped like Mickey Mouse to be a decorative (aka décor) Mickey. Disneyland is loaded with decorative Mickeys. You'll find obvious images of Mickey Mouse on items such as manhole covers, displays in shop windows, and restaurant menus. I do not include these ubiquitous and sometimes changing images in this book unless they are unique or hard to spot.

Hidden Mickeys can change or be accidentally removed over time, by the processes of nature or by the continual cleaning and refurbishing that goes on at Disneyland. For example, a classic Mickey on an outside duct at *Muppet*Vision 3D* was painted over and is no longer with us. Cast Members themselves sometimes create or remove Hidden Mickeys.

My Selection Process

I trust you've concluded by now that Hidden Mickey Science is an evolving specialty. Which raises the question, how did I choose the more than 480 Hidden Mickeys in the scavenger hunts in this guide? I compiled my list of Hidden Mickeys from all the resources to which I had access: my own sightings, sightings sent to me by others (see "Acknowledgements," page 139, websites, books, and Cast Members. (Cast Members in each specific area usually—but not always!—know where some Hidden Mickeys are located.) Then I embarked on my verification hunts, asking for help along the way from generous Disney Cast Members. I have included only those Hidden Mickeys I could personally verify.

Furthermore, some Hidden Mickeys are visible only intermittently or only from certain vantage points in ride vehicles. I don't generally include these Mickeys, unless I feel that adequate descriptions will allow anyone to find them. So the scavenger hunts include only those images I believe to be recognizable as Hidden Mickeys and visible to the general touring guest. It is quite likely, though, that one or more of the Hidden Mickeys described in this book will disappear over time.

I'll try to let you know when I discover that a Hidden Mickey has disappeared for good by posting the information on my website:

www.HiddenMickeyGuy.com

If you find one missing before I do, I hope you'll let me know by emailing me care of my website.

I have enjoyed finding each and every Hidden Mickey in this book. I'm certain I'll find more as time goes by, and I hope you can spot new Hidden Mickeys during your visit.

So put on some comfortable walking shoes and experience the Disneyland Resort like you never have before!

Happy Hunting!

— *Steve Barrett*

CHAPTER 2

Disneyland Park Scavenger Hunt

•••••••••••••••••••••••••••••••••••

★ Arrive at the entrance turnstiles (with your admission ticket) 45 minutes before the opening time for early entry (if you're eligible) or 45 minutes before official opening time if it's a non-early entry day.

★ Search for one or more of the following Hidden Mickeys in the **security bag check area** if you have plenty of time before the park opens; otherwise, look for them when you leave the park.

Clue 1: Study the signs above you for a classic Mickey on a key chain.
4 points

Clue 2: Now search the signs for a classic Mickey on a ride vehicle.
4 points

Clue 3: Find Mickey ears on Timon and Pumbaa in two different signs.
4 points for spotting both

Clue 4: Locate two more signs with Mickey ears.
4 points for finding both

Clue 5: As soon as you pass through the **entrance turnstiles**, look around for a classic Mickey.
3 points

★ Now ride **Peter Pan's Flight**.

Clue 6: At the beginning of the ride, read two names in blocks below you.
4 points for finding both

Clue 7: Look for Mickey in Big Ben.
5 points

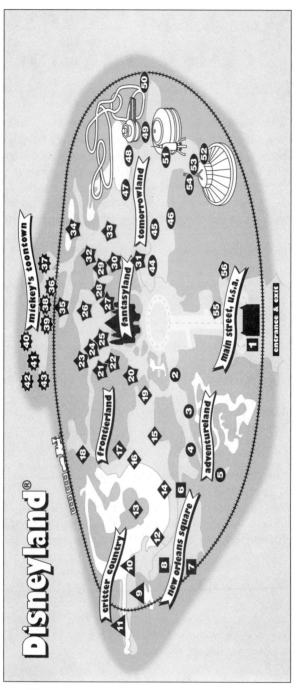

1 Disneyland Railroad, Entrance

adventureland
2 Enchanted Tiki Room
3 Jungle Cruise
4 Tarzan's Treehouse™
5 Indiana Jones™ Adventure

new orleans square
6 Pirates of the Caribbean
7 Disneyland Railroad
8 Haunted Mansion

critter country
9 Splash Mountain
10 Davy Crockett's Explorer Canoes
11 The Many Adventures of Winnie the Pooh

frontierland
12 Raft to Tom Sawyer Island
13 Pirate's Lair on Tom Sawyer Island

14 Fantasmic!
15 The Golden Horseshoe Stage
16 Mark Twain Riverboat and Sailing Ship Columbia
17 Big Thunder Mountain Railroad
18 Big Thunder Ranch
19 Frontierland Shootin' Exposition

fantasyland
20 Fantasy Faire
21 Pinocchio's Daring Journey
22 Snow White's Scary Adventures
23 Casey Jr. Circus Train
24 King Arthur Carrousel
25 Sleeping Beauty Castle Walkthrough
26 Dumbo the Flying Elephant
27 Peter Pan's Flight

28 Mr. Toad's Wild Ride
29 Mad Tea Party
30 Alice in Wonderland
31 Pixie Hollow
32 Storybook Land Canal Boats
33 Matterhorn Bobsleds
34 "it's a small world"
35 Fantasyland Theatre

mickey's toontown
36 Disneyland Railroad
37 Roger Rabbit's Car Toon Spin
38 Goofy's Playhouse
39 Donald's Boat
40 Minnie's House
41 Mickey's House
42 Chip 'n Dale Treehouse
43 Gadget's Go Coaster

tomorrowland
44 Astro Orbitor
45 Buzz Lightyear Astro Blasters
46 Star Tours — The Adventures Continue
47 Finding Nemo Submarine Voyage
48 Disneyland Monorail
49 Autopia
50 Disneyland Railroad
51 Innoventions
52 Space Mountain
53 Magic Eye Theater
54 Starcade

main street, u.s.a.
55 Main Street Cinema
56 Disneyland Story...
Mr. Lincoln

19

★ Outside *Peter Pan's Flight* ...

Clue 8: Search high for a Hidden Mickey.
3 points

★ Then walk toward the **Matterhorn Bobsleds** in Fantasyland. Observe the side of the mountain that faces *"it's a small world."*

Clue 9: Locate a Mickey clearing in the snow.
5 points

★ Line up for the *Bobsleds* ride in the right-hand queue.

Clue 10: Study the right *Bobsleds* queue area for a Hidden Mickey on a coat of arms.
4 points

Clue 11: While on the ride, stay alert for a Hidden Mickey in an ice cave.
5 bonus points

Clue 12: Walk to the smoking area on the Tomorrowland side of the Matterhorn and find Nemo!
4 points

Clue 13: Stroll toward Tomorrowland and search for a Mickey-shaped hole on the outside of Matterhorn Mountain.
4 points

★ Head next to **Buzz Lightyear Astro Blasters** in Tomorrowland.

Clue 14: Search for two Mickey continents along the entrance queue.
6 points for finding both

Clue 15: Find two classic (three-circle) Hidden Mickeys along the entrance queue.
6 points for finding both

Clue 16: On the ride, watch to your left for a classic Mickey on a block.
3 points

Clue 17: Now spot an oblong satellite on the wall with a Hidden Mickey on its side.
4 points

Clue 18: After you step off the ride vehicle, search for a side-profile Mickey on the wall.
2 points

Clue 19: Find two classic Mickeys in the same area.
2 points each

★ Check into **Star Tours—The Adventures Continue**.

Clue 20: Along the entrance queue, spot a Hidden Mickey near C-3PO.
3 points

Clue 21: Now wait for a shadow Hidden Mickey in a video on a wall display along the entrance queue.
4 points

Clue 22: Stay alert for another shadow Mickey image on the wall to your right along the entrance queue.
5 points

Clue 23: Next, study the entrance queue luggage scanner for Mickey and other Disney characters and images.
5 points total for finding Mickey and two or more other Disney images

★ Go to *Space Mountain* and get a FASTPASS for later.

★ If the wait is 20 minutes or less, line up at the **Pixie Hollow** meet and greet area.

Clue 24: At the end of the waiting queue, don't overlook a classic Mickey.
4 points

★ Get in line for **Mr. Toad's Wild Ride**.

Clue 25: Find a tiny Mickey along the inside entrance queue.
4 points

Clue 26: At the beginning of the ride, stare at a right-hand door for a tiny dark Mickey in the door's stained glass.
5 points

Clue 27: Search for Mickey in beer foam.
4 points

Clue 28: Stay alert for Sherlock Holmes in a window. (A Hidden Surprise, not a Hidden Mickey!)
5 points

★ Return to **Space Mountain** during your FAST-PASS window and walk up the entrance queue. You can skip the ride if you want; there were no Hidden Mickeys in it last time I checked.

Clue 29: Find Mickey along the entrance queue.
2 points

Clue 30: See anything on the ride vehicles?
2 points

★ Now get a FASTPASS for *Indiana Jones Adventure*.

★ Wander over to New Orleans Square and hop on **Pirates of the Caribbean**.

Clue 31: During the first part of your boat ride, study the water for Mickey.
5 points

Clue 32: Stay alert for Mickey on a chair by a bed.
4 points

Clue 33: After you pass the skeleton in bed, look back for an image of Goofy.
5 points

Clue 34: If Davy Jones appears in the mist, check him out for a classic Mickey.
5 bonus points

Clue 35: In the first fight scene, spot a classic Mickey on a wall.
5 points

Clue 36: Near the end of the ride, study the armor on the wall for a classic Mickey.
5 points

Clue 37: After you exit the boat, look around for a classic Mickey on a door.
2 points

Clue 38: Study the outside railings in New Orleans Square for some famous initials (another Hidden Surprise).
5 points for both names

★ Turn left at the exit to enjoy **Haunted Mansion**.

Clue 39: Look high along the mansion walls for a Hidden Mickey.
3 points

Clue 40: Search for Mickey in the wallpaper.
3 points

Clue 41: While on the ride, can you find Donald Duck?
4 points

Clue 42: If snow is in the ballroom, find Mickey!
5 points

Clue 43: As you ride, keep alert for plates and saucers.
3 points

Clue 44: In the attic, look for a clock with a Hidden Mickey.
5 points

★ Mosey on over to **The Golden Horseshoe** in Frontierland. You can order a counter-service lunch and, if the timing is right, catch a great show on its stage (check your your Times Guide for show times, and while you're at it, plan to enjoy a 2:30 p.m. or later showing of *Mickey and the Magical Map*).

Clue 45: Check around the stage for a classic Mickey.
3 points

Clue 46: Now study the wall paintings for a Hidden Mickey.
3 points

★ Walk to Adventureland during your next FASTPASS window and enjoy **Indiana Jones Adventure**.

Clue 47: Study the walls of the standby queue for Mickey's "initials."
4 points

Clue 48: In the circular room with the rope you can pull on, search for a stone disk (propped upright) with a tiny classic Mickey. (Note: This image is becoming more faint with time and may disappear.)
5 points

Clue 49: Now look up for another classic Mickey in the same room.
3 points

Clue 50: Find a large classic Mickey in the room with the video screen.
4 points

Clue 51: Toward the end of the video room, look up and say "hi" to Eeyore!
5 points

Clue 52: When you leave the video room, peer into an office to spot Mickey.
3 points

Clue 53: After the ride starts, gaze up into Mara's huge face for a classic Mickey.
3 points

Clue 54: When your vehicle enters the Mummy Room, find a Mickey Mouse hat.
5 points

★ Get a FASTPASS for *Big Thunder Mountain Railroad*.

★ Hop on the **Disneyland Railroad** train at the New Orleans Square station and ride around the park. You can exit at New Orleans Square station and walk to your next destination.

Clue 55: As you ride along, search the scenery on the right side of the train for a Hidden Mickey.
5 points

Clue 56: Now keep your eyes peeled for a Hidden Mickey in grapes.
3 points

★ Ride **Mark Twain Riverboat** or **Sailing Ship Columbia**.

Clue 57: While on board, scour the river for a classic Mickey in the water.
3 points

Clue 58: Seek out the *Mark Twain Riverboat* (if you haven't already). Concentrate on the front of the ship to spot a Hidden Mickey.
2 points

Clue 59: Search for Mickey Mouse in a painting near the *Mark Twain Riverboat* loading dock.
5 points

★ Walk to **Big Thunder Mountain Railroad** in Frontierland during your FASTPASS window.

Clue 60: While on the ride, search for three gears that form a classic Mickey.
3 points

Clue 61: Find Mickey at the exit.
3 points

★ Cross over to Critter Country. Get a FASTPASS for *Splash Mountain* to ride later.

★ Float on the *Raft to* **Tom Sawyer Island**.

Clue 62: On Tom Sawyer Island, seek out a cavern entrance with a classic Mickey.
3 points

Clue 63: Study the treasure in the *Pirate's Lair* for a classic Mickey.
4 points

★ Return by raft to Frontierland.

★ Walk to Tomorrowland. Go to *Finding Nemo Submarine Voyage* and then look for the *Monorail* exit to find the **elevator for the Disneyland Monorail**.

Clue 64: First go up to the *Monorail* exit deck to spot a Hidden Mickey near the water below you. (Note: This Hidden Mickey comes and goes.)
4 bonus points

Clue 65: Now search for Mickey near the elevator on the ground level.
5 points

★ Ask a Cast Member for permission to enter the **Marine Observation Outpost** at the right side of the *Finding Nemo Submarine Voyage* entrance queue.

Clue 66: Look around inside for a Hidden Mickey.
4 points

★ Go to **Innoventions**. If the *ASIMO* show, the *Dream Home*, and the rotating murals on Innoventions' outside walls are still there (*Innoventions* was in rehab mode when I last visited), search for some Hidden Mickeys.

★ Check your Times Guide or ask a Cast Member when the next *ASIMO* show is scheduled and factor it into your itinerary. Then stop by the large blue globe standing on a floor of small beads (some call them "pebbles") under glass.

Clue 67: Stand in front of the middle of the globe and watch the images on the globe for Mickey.
3 points

Clue 68: Facing the front middle of the globe, look down below your feet and find three beads stuck together to form Mickey.
5 points

Clue 69: Walk to your left close to the wall and spot another Mickey formed by three beads stuck together.
5 points

★ Now enjoy the **Dream Home** and spot a few Hidden Mickeys.

Clue 70: Don't miss Mickey's shadow at the front door!
3 points

Clue 71: Check out the balloons in the window.
3 points

Clue 72: Search both outside and just inside the front door.
3 points total for finding Mickey in both areas

Clue 73: Look down for Mickey as you walk through the Dream Home.
2 points

Clue 74: Find two images of Mickey in the boy's bedroom.
4 points for finding both

Clue 75: Check the inside murals for classic Mickeys.
4 points

Clue 76: Study a wall in the **ASIMO robot show area** for a Hidden Mickey.
3 points

Clue 77: Find Mickey near the computer in the *ASI-MO* show area.
3 points

Clue 78: Watch the *ASIMO* show video for a Hidden Mickey.
4 points

★ Exit *Innoventions*.

Clue 79: Study the rotating murals on the outside walls for two Hidden Mickeys.
4 points for spotting both

Clue 80: Continue studying the rotating murals for another Hidden Character.
4 points

★ Walk along the entrance queue for **Autopia**.

Clue 81: Find a classic Mickey on the cars.
3 points

★ Walk to the **Fantasyland Theatre** at your chosen time for a showing of *Mickey and the Magical Map*.

Clue 82: Scan the overhead stage border. You might find Mickey!
4 points

Clue 83: Study the left side of the stage for a classic Mickey in a window.
5 points

Clue 84: Watch the show as a black splotch turns into a classic Mickey, just for a second.
5 points

Clue 85: Observe the rear screen for a floating Hidden Mickey.
3 points

Clue 86: Keep looking for Mickey inside some bubbles!
4 points

★ Cross Fantasyland to **Fantasy Faire**.

Clue 87: Search for a classic Hidden Mickey inside the Music Box.
5 points

Clue 88: Now scan the crowd inside the Music Box for Disney Characters.
5 points for five or more

★ Ride **Splash Mountain** during your FASTPASS window.

Clue 89: Check out the outside entrance queue for a tiny Mickey.
5 points

Clue 90: Search for a classic Mickey along the inside queue.
3 points

Clue 91: Look up for Mickey just before the big drop.
4 points

Clue 92: While on the ride, stay alert for a picture of Mickey on the wall. (Note: This Mickey image may come and go.)
4 bonus points

★ Make time in your schedule for the **afternoon parade**. (Note: The parade floats change from time to time but usually include Hidden Mickeys in their decoration.) The antique Grand Marshal automobile sometimes leads the parade.

Clue 93: Search this antique car for several Hidden Mickeys.
5 bonus points for finding three or more

★ If you're up for a mild climb through an imaginative tree, check out **Tarzan's Treehouse** in Adventure-land.

Clue 94: Study the room with the ship's wheel for a Hidden Mickey near the floor.
3 points

Clue 95: In this same room, look for a Hidden Mickey on the wall.
3 points

Clue 96: Along your walk through the tree, two characters from *Beauty and the Beast* make an appearance.
4 points for finding both

★ Check inside the **Indiana Jones Adventure Outpost** shop.

Clue 97: Find a Hidden Mickey on a wall inside.
3 points

★ Stroll toward the **Enchanted Tiki Room**.

Clue 98: Observe the shields outside near the exit to find a classic Mickey.
3 points

★ Enjoy **"Captain EO"** in Tomorrowland

Clue 99: Observe Captain EO's ship.
3 points

★ Now stroll over to **The Many Adventures of Winnie the Pooh** in Critter Country.

Clue 100: Study the "Hunny Pot" vehicles for a classic Mickey.
2 points

Clue 101: Just after the ride starts, be aware of a classic Mickey in the wood.
5 points

Clue 102: Locate Mickey ears near the sleeping Pooh.
5 points

Clue 103: After the Heffalumps and Woozles dream room, search high behind you for a Hidden Surprise. (It's not a Hidden Mickey, but it's a cool image that everyone should enjoy.)
5 points

Clue 104: Look for classic Mickey circles near Heffalumps.
3 points

★ Turn right and walk to the **Briar Patch** store in Critter Country (near *Splash Mountain*).

Clue 105: Look inside the store for a Hidden Mickey.
3 points

★ Amble over to **Big Thunder Ranch**.

Clue 106: Spot a Hidden Mickey near the entrance.
4 points

Clue 107: Don't miss Mickey atop a big pile!
4 points

★ Go to **Casey Jr. Circus Train** in Fantasyland.

Clue 108: Examine the conductor's cabin for Mickey. (You can spot this Hidden Mickey without riding the train.)
3 points

★ Walk to the **Storybook Land Canal Boats** ride and study the boats before you board and after you exit your boat.

Clue 109: A Hidden Mickey is on the back of the "Daisy" boat.
3 points

Clue 110: Study the "Flora" boat for a Hidden Mickey.
4 points

Clue 111: A bluebird on the back of the "Snow White" boat is looking at this Hidden Mickey.
5 points

Clue 112: Don't forget the "Wendy" boat's Hidden Mickey!
2 points

Clue 113: While on the boat ride, search for a Hidden Mickey above a village.
3 points

★ In Adventureland, check out **Jungle Cruise**.

Clue 114: Glance up outside the entrance for a Hidden Character.
2 points

Clue 115: From your boat, look behind the dancing and chanting natives for a *Lion King* image. (This isn't a Hidden Mickey, but it's a cool Hidden Surprise!)
5 points

Clue 116: Search the side of the river for Donald Duck's face on a native.
4 points

★ Stop by Bengal Barbecue or Royal Street Veranda for dinner. Be sure to note the times for *Fantasmic!* and the *Fireworks* shows and fit them into your plans. If two *Fantasmic!* shows are scheduled, the later show will be less congested.

★ Go to **Pinocchio's Daring Journey** in Fantasyland.

Clue 117: Watch the floor to spot a yellow Hidden Mickey.
4 points

Clue 118: Check the popcorn stand on your right for a classic Mickey.
4 points

Clue 119: Look for a Hidden Mickey near a ship.
5 points

★ Step over to **Snow White's Scary Adventures**.

Clue 120: Find Mickey at the loading dock.
3 points

Clue 121: On the ride, watch for a classic Mickey on an animal.
3 points

★ Queue up to ride **Alice in Wonderland**.

Clue 122: On the ride, search for a classic Mickey in red paint.
4 points

★ Walk to **Mickey's Toontown**

(Note: You'll find many Mickey shapes throughout Toontown. I don't include the larger, more obvious Mickey images as Hidden Mickeys; they're more properly designated décor Mickeys.)

Clue 123: Look for Mickey near the entrance to Mickey's Toontown.
2 points

★ Saunter over to **Minnie's House**.

Clue 124: Mickey is hiding in the first room inside.
3 points

Clue 125: Mickey is also hiding in Minnie's kitchen.
2 points

★ Search for Mickey outside Minnie's House.

Clue 126: Look near the big blue doors.
5 points

★ Stroll over to **Mickey's House**.

Clue 127: See anything in his front door?
1 point

Clue 128: Glance down for Mickey.
1 point

Clues 129 and 130: Look inside a glass-fronted book-case for some Hidden Mickeys.
3 points total for finding one on each of two books

Clue 131: Stare at other books in the first room.
3 points

Clues 132 and 133: In the piano room, search for two Hidden Mickeys in a bookcase.
2 points each; 4 points total

Clue 134: Find classic Mickeys and other Hidden Characters in the piano.
5 points for a Hidden Mickey and two other characters

Clue 135: Something's atop the piano.
2 points

Clue 136: Look for Mickey on a drum.
2 points

Clue 137: Spot Mickey on a clock.
2 points

Clue 138: Pay attention to a special mirror inside Mickey's Movie Barn (the room in *Mickey's House* where you wait to meet Mickey in person).
4 points

Clue 139: Study Donald's workbench for a paint-splotch Hidden Mickey.
4 points

Clue 140: Also in Mickey's Movie Barn, watch the countdown screen.
4 points

Clue 141: Once outside, admire Mickey's car and find Hidden Mickeys.
3 points for one or more

Clue 142: Search for Mickey on a lamp.
3 points

★ Get in line for **Gadget's Go Coaster**. The Hidden Mickeys here are along the queue. You can skip the actual ride if you want; just ask to exit when you reach the loading area.

Clue 143: Stay alert for at least three rock classic Mickeys in the queue walls.
3 points each; 9 points total

Clue 144: Gaze around the vehicle loading area for a Hidden Mickey.
4 points

★ If you're in Mickey's Toontown when **Clarabelle's Frozen Yogurt** closes, look around for a Hidden Mickey. (Ask a Cast Member when Clarabelle's will close; you may need to return later.)

Clue 145: At closing, a Hidden Mickey appears.
2 points

Clue 146: Find two more at the **Post Office**.
4 points for finding both

Clue 147: Ring the doorbell at the **Toontown Fire Department** and watch for a Hidden Mickey.
5 points

Clue 148: Study the roof of the **Fireworks Factory** for a small, blue classic Mickey.
5 points

★ Return to Fantasyland and relax on a gentle boat ride at **"it's a small world."**

Clue 149: Look for Mickey along the entrance queue.
3 points

Clue 150: Stay alert for Hidden Characters.
5 points for spotting five or more

Clue 151: Study a balloon above you for a Hidden Mickey bear shadow.
4 points

Clue 152: Watch the ceiling for a Hidden Mickey.
3 points

★ Stroll over to **King Arthur Carrousel**. Find the Hidden Mickeys from outside the carrousel.

Clue 153: Check out the horses for Hidden Mickeys.
2 points each; 4 points total

★ Cross Fantasyland to the **Mad Hatter** shop, not far from the *Mad Tea Party* attraction.

Clue 154: Search around inside the shop for a Hidden cat.
5 points

Clue 155: Spot Hidden Mickeys outside the shop.
2 points each for two Hidden Mickeys

★ Back near Sleeping Beauty Castle, locate the **Castle Heraldry Shoppe**.

Clue 156: Find two Hidden Mickeys outside the store.
5 points for finding both

★ Walk to the rear of Tomorrowland to **Redd Rockett's Pizza Port** to find another Hidden Mickey.

Clue 157: Search around inside the restaurant for a Hidden Mickey.
3 points

★ Retrace your steps to **The Star Trader** shop (not far from *Star Tours*).

Clue 158: Glance inside The Star Trader for small classic Mickeys in poles.
2 points

Clue 159: Now find two different Hidden Mickeys on merchandise bins.
3 points for finding both types

★ Step over to the **Little Green Men Store Command** (next to *Buzz Lightyear Astro Blasters*).

Clue 160: Look for Mickey on a sign.
4 points

★ Walk **toward the central hub**.

Clue 161: Study the spheres of the *Astro Orbitor*.
2 points

★ Cross the central hub to the **walkway to Frontierland**.

Clue 162: Look for a Hidden Mickey along the entrance walkway to Frontierland.
3 points

★ Stop in at the **Frontierland Shootin' Exposition**.

Clue 163: Spot a Hidden Mickey toward the front of the shootin' area.
3 points

★ Enter the **Pioneer Mercantile** shop.

Clue 164: Examine the wall for Mickey.
3 points

Clue 165: Locate Mickey near a cashier.
3 points

★ Walk to the **Rancho del Zocalo Restaurante**.

Clue 166: Search inside the restaurant for a classic Mickey in wood.
4 points

★ Go left to the **River Belle Terrace** restaurant.

Clue 167: Find a Hidden Mickey on a chair inside.
3 points

37

Clue 168: Now look around the restaurant for a classic Mickey in a painting.
4 points

★ Return to **Main Street, U.S.A.**

Clue 169: Check inside the **Plaza Inn** restaurant.
3 points

★ Enter the **Photo Supply Company**.

Clue 170: Look for Mickey on a camera.
3 points

★ Stand outside the **Silhouette Studio**.

Clue 171: Spot a Hidden Mickey in a display window.
4 points

Clue 172: Find a Hidden Mickey outside on a **fruit cart**.
4 points

★ Stroll down Main Street to **Main Street Cinema**. Walk inside.

Clue 173: Look around for some Hidden Mickeys.
3 points for one or more

Clue 174: Outside Main Street Cinema, search for two Hidden Mickeys.
2 points each; 4 points total

★ Find more Mickeys at the **Main Street Magic Shop**.

Clue 175: Spot Mickey on a display shelf.
3 points

Clue 176: Glance high for Mickey!
4 points

Clue 177: Locate a classic Mickey outside the shop.
3 points

★ Walk toward the Castle to the **Penny Arcade**.

Clue 178: Don't miss the small Hidden Mickey on a game machine inside the Penny Arcade!
4 points

★ Approach the **Gibson Girl Ice Cream Parlor**.

Clue 179: Admire the outside windows for a Hidden Mickey.
5 points

Clue 180: Look up for a Hidden Mickey.
2 points

★ Stroll to the **Emporium** store.

Clue 181: Admire the outside window displays for classic Mickeys.
2 points total for one or more

Clue 182: Inside an entrance at the end of the store closest to City Hall, search for Mickey in a painting on the wall.
5 points

Clue 183: Find a room in the store with toy merchandise and look for a train circling a track overhead. Wait for a lighted Hidden Mickey to appear!
5 points

★ Cross Main Street to the **Mad Hatter**.

Clue 184: Scan all the windows outside the store for a Hidden Mickey.
5 points

★ Walk to the **Main Street Station** of the **Disneyland Railroad**.

Clue 185: Wait for the trains and study their forward sections for Hidden Mickeys.
5 points total for one or more

★ Watch the **Fantasmic!** show for a Hidden Mickey.

Clue 186: Be alert for a Hidden Mickey on the water screen.
5 points

★ Don't miss the nighttime **fireworks show**!

Clue 187: Watch the sky during the fireworks show for a Hidden Mickey.
5 bonus points

★ Exit Disneyland Park.

Clue 188: In the **entrance plaza**, look for Mickey at your feet.
3 points

Clue 189: Spot Mickey at the tops and bottoms of some of the poles.
4 points for spotting Mickey in both places

Now total your score and see how you did.

Total Points for Disneyland Park =

How'd You Do?

Up to 269 points – Bronze
270 to 537 points – Silver
538 points and over – Gold
672 points – Perfect Score

(If you earned bonus points by spotting Hidden Mickeys in the *Matterhorn Bobsleds'* ice cave, *Pirates of the Caribbean*, the picture on the wall in *Splash Mountain* or on the Grand Marshal's car during the afternoon parade, you may have done even better.)

Notes

**Caution:
Don't peek at this
section unless you
really want help!**

Security Bag Check Area

Hint 1: Various pictures of characters from *The Lion King* hang above you. On the picture with the warning "Hold On To Your Gear!" a small key chain flies through the air behind Timon and Pumbaa as they ride a roller coaster. A tiny black classic Mickey is on the blue part of the key chain. (You may need to wander around the security area to find the picture.)

Hint 2: On the sign warning "Let The Cubs Decide If They Want To Ride," a small white classic Mickey is above the word "Cubs" on a blue ride vehicle occupied by Timon and Pumbaa.

Hint 3: Timon and Pumbaa are wearing Mickey ears on the sign that says "Keep Arms, Hooves, Tusks and Tails inside the Vehicle" as well as on the sign that says "Be Aware, It's a Jungle Out There!"

Hint 4: In a sign that says "Stay On Your Feet, It's Not a Seat," Timon wears Mickey ears and another Mickey hat flies through the air. In the sign that says "Paws Behind the Line," Mickey ears fly through the air above a cloud near a pink castle.

Entrance

Hint 5: As soon as you enter Disneyland, turn around and spot the classic Mickey speaker grid on the utility box next to the entrance turnstile. (Note: The ticket attendant may be blocking your view.)

Fantasyland

- Peter Pan's Flight

Hint 6: As you walk through the entrance queue, lean over the rail and look into the first scene (the bedroom) of the ride. Alphabet blocks are stacked and scattered on the floor. On the ride, as your vehicle soars over the bedroom, look down at the blocks and find these words: "DISNEY" (spelled as "D13NEY") and "PETER PAN." (Cast Members sometimes change these blocks around.)

Hint 7: As you fly over London, a side-view Mickey silhouette hides in a top window on the left side of Big Ben. Look back at the window as you pass by the clock tower.

Hint 8: Inside a high window to the left of the entrance to the attraction, classic Mickeys are on the bottom of a plush bear's paws. The paws are at the lower right, next to the window curtain.

- Matterhorn Bobsleds

Hint 9: Admire the Matterhorn from in front of Le Petit Chalet shop near *"it's a small world."* About two-thirds the way up the side of the mountain, a clearing in the snow forms a classic Mickey, tilted to the left.

Hint 10: A tiny black classic Mickey is in the middle of a red and white coat of arms at

the rear of the right queue. The Mickey is on a red triangle at the bottom of a white pole.

Hint 11: To your left during the first part of the ride, on the floor of the first ice cave, where you will see expedition equipment and glowing crystals, a rope between the ice crystals and the crates is coiled into a classic Mickey. (Note: This Hidden Mickey comes and goes.)

Hint 12: Exit *Matterhorn Bobsleds* on the Tomorrowland side to find a Hidden Nemo traced on the side of a wooden electrical box. It's across the walkway from the Matterhorn exit at an entrance to a smoking area.

Tomorrowland

- view of Matterhorn Mountain

Hint 13: A large black classic Mickey hole hides in the side of the Matterhorn Mountain. You can see it from various vantage points in Tomorrowland.

- Buzz Lightyear Astro Blasters

Hint 14: As soon as you enter the building, look for two "Ska-densii" planets with side-profile "continent" Mickeys along the right side wall.

Hint 15: Two upside-down classic Mickeys appear in the large "Planets of the Galactic Alliance" mural on the wall of the entrance queue. One is located at about the "10 o'clock" position in the planet named K'lifooel'ch; it is made of small green spheres. The other is made of white spheres and hides on the right side of the mural above the words "K'tleendon Kan Cluster."

Hint 16: A classic Mickey is etched on a block in the first show room to the left of the vehicle, just past a large rotating wheel and left of a row of target batteries.

Hint 17: Watch the wall for an oblong satellite (called "Green Planet" on the queue mural) with an antenna on top and green swirls on the side. Three swirls in the middle of its side form a tilted classic Hidden Mickey.

Hint 18: A side-profile Mickey hides on a "Ska-densii" planet's continent on a right wall mural across from the photo-viewing area. If it looks familiar, it's because you see the same Hidden Mickeys (as well as the two below) on an entrance-queue mural.

Hint 19: On this same mural on the right wall along the inside exit, look for K'lifooel'ch, the planet formed of many small green spheres. A classic Mickey lies along the outer edge of K'lifooel'ch at about the "10 o'clock" location (other classic Mickey spheres are also part of this planet) and an upside-down classic Mickey is formed by three white spheres at the middle right of the mural, above the words "K'tleendon Kan Cluster."

- Star Tours—The Adventures Continue

Hint 20: Circles create a Mickey hat with ears on the upper part of the control panel behind C-3PO's head.

Hint 21: In a wall display along the entrance queue, the silhouette of R2-D2 appears several times in a continuous video loop of moving shadow figures. At one point, R2-D2 sprouts satellite ears that rotate into round "Mickey ears" for a few seconds.

Hint 22: Along the right side of the entrance queue ramps, in the second room with the luggage inspection, a small droid casts a shadow of Mickey ears on the wall.

Hint 23: Along the entrance queue, a robot watches a continuous scan of luggage moving along a conveyor belt. You can spot images of a plush Mickey Mouse and a plush Goofy, along with images of Buzz Lightyear, Aladdin's lamp, a Sorcerer Mickey hat, a Mr. Incredible shirt, Madame Leota's crystal ball, and others.

Fantasyland

- Pixie Hollow

Hint 24: At the end of the *Pixie Hollow* waiting queue is a signpost that reads "Fairies Welcome." A classic Mickey is carved out of bark on the front of the signpost, near the bottom.

- Mr. Toad's Wild Ride

Hint 25: On the large statue of Mr. Toad, to the left of the inside entrance queue, tiny red splotches can be seen in the lower part of both corneas (above the white part of the eyes). Both splotches resemble classic Hidden Mickeys, but the one in Mr. Toad's left eye (as you face the statue, it's the eye on the right) is more convincing.

Hint 26: At the beginning of the ride, on the third set of doors that your car drives through, you'll see the head and ears of a tiny dark Mickey. It's in the right door's lower left panel, in the bottom left-most triangle of stained glass. It's hard to spot!

Hint 27: In Winky's Pub, about halfway through the ride, an upside-down classic Mickey appears in the foam in the top left corner of the left mug (as you face the scene) above Winky's hand.

Hint 28: The silhouette of Sherlock Holmes can be found on the second-floor window above the Constabulary door. It's in the city room (the room with the fountain) just after you pass the bartender who spins the mugs. Once you leave the pub room, look directly to the left and up a little and you'll see Sherlock. (He's not a Disney character, but this is one cool hidden image nonetheless.)

Tomorrowland

- Space Mountain

Hint 29: Mickey ears appear on the right side of the safety video in which you're asked to place "loose possessions in the storage pouch in front of you."

Hint 30: The speakers on the back of the ride-vehicle seats form classic Mickeys.

New Orleans Square

- *Pirates of the Caribbean*

Hint 31: As you drift past the Blue Bayou Restaurant seating area, a classic Mickey appears in the water to the right of your boat. It's formed by the last set of three lily pads that you pass before you enter the caverns.

Hint 32: To the left of your boat, a classic Mickey hides on the upper back of the chair near the near the bed where the pirate skeleton is lying.

Hint 33: Just after you float by the skeleton in bed on your left, look back at the ceiling of the cavern behind you for a large rock that juts out over the water above you. The shape of the rock resembles Goofy.

Hint 34: Look for the sheet of mist in front of your boat. If Davy Jones appears (as opposed to Blackbeard), stare at the left side of his hat (his right side, viewer's left). Below and to the left of the bottom of the "V" at the front of his hat, three tiny gold balls form a classic Mickey.

Hint 35: In the first battle scene, there are three cannonball impact craters on the upper part of the fort wall on the right side of your boat. This crater classic Mickey is below the middle cannon and best seen if you turn around to view it as you are passing by the fort.

Hint 36: This classic Mickey is to the left of your boat in the last room, where pieces of armor hang from the wall. Look for the gold breastplate, usually the rightmost armor breastplate, with a coat of arms emblem. In the center of that emblem are classic Mickey circles. (Note: The items in

48

the armor display are moved around at times. The last time I visited, I saw the gold breastplate on the wall just before Jack Sparrow's treasure room at the end of the ride.)

Hint 37: On the right side as you exit, and before you reach the street outside, a classic Mickey-shaped lock adorns a back door to the Pieces of Eight shop.

- New Orleans Square

Hint 38: Walt and Roy Disney's gold stylized initials are in the blue railing above the Royal Street Veranda.

- Haunted Mansion

Hint 39: As soon as you walk through the front door along the entrance queue, go to any of the candlestick holders on the wall and, with your back to the wall, look up from underneath to spot a classic Mickey effect.

Hint 40: Large circles form classic Mickeys in the wallpaper of the Art Gallery after you exit the Stretching Room.

Hint 41: As you pass by the "endless hallway" in your Doom Buggy, check out the back of the purple chair for an abstract Donald Duck. Near the top of the chair, you can see his cap, which sits above his distorted eyes, face and bill. (Note: The chair location may change at times.)

Hint 42: In the Ballroom scene, "snow" may dust the floor at the right rear of the room. When it does, a classic Mickey formed of snow is usually somewhere in the snowdrift.

Hint 43: During the Ballroom scene, look down at the place settings near the center of the dining table. You'll see two small saucers and one larger plate forming a classic Mickey. The Cast Members move this Hidden Mickey around at times.

49

Hint 44: After the ballroom scene, look to the right as soon as you enter the attic. Find the clock on a bureau to the right of the round portrait of a bride and groom and just to the right of a bright orange and blue lamp. A brown classic Mickey hides behind the pendulum of the clock.

Frontierland

- The Golden Horseshoe

Hint 45: Walk toward the front of the stage and find a grating vent in the center of the lower front wall. Start at the lower right hole in the grate. Then look up and diagonally left one hole to spot a classic Mickey hole in the grating.

Hint 46: Look for the "Hall of Fame" picture on the left wall lower level. Sideways gold classic Mickeys hide at the middle sides of the frame around Betty Taylor's picture.

Adventureland

- Indiana Jones Adventure

Hint 47: Across from the first drinking fountains in the inside standby queue, Mickey's initials, "M M" in Mara script, are on the left wall, just above a horizontal crack in the wall.

Hint 48: On the side of a bamboo structure just opposite the hanging rope, a large painted stone disk has a tiny light blue classic Hidden Mickey symbol on the lower right edge of the outer circle of symbols. (Note: This image is becoming fainter with time and may disappear.)

Hint 49: On the ceiling, Mara's giant nose is a classic Mickey.

Hint 50: When you enter the room showing the video on a screen, study the left wall for a large classic Hidden Mickey between the last two lights on the wall.

Hint 51: *Indiana Jones Adventure* was built over a previous Eeyore (cast) parking lot. As a tribute to the past, an original white parking sign in the shape of Eeyore was placed in the video room, high up in the rafters. To spot it, go to the end of the video room, turn around, and look up to the left of the projector. If you can't find it, ask a nearby Cast Member for help.

Hint 52: In an office just past the video room, Mickey and Minnie Mouse are pictured on a partially visible magazine page. The magazine is on a desktop. (Note: These magazine images are moved around and may not be visible at times.)

Hint 53: Shortly after the ride starts, look at Mara's face for a (not quite perfect) classic Mickey formed by her nostrils and the tip of her nose.

Hint 54: As soon as your vehicle turns a corner and enters the Mummy Room, look left for a skeleton wearing a Mickey Mouse hat. Let's hope the hat stays put!

New Orleans Square

- Disneyland Railroad

Hint 55: On the right side of the *Disneyland Railroad* train, between the New Orleans Square and Mickey's Toontown stations, a coiled rope lying on a wooden deck forms a classic Mickey. Look for the rope Mickey near a small shed, in a scene behind *Big Thunder Ranch*. (Note: This rope Mickey is sometimes temporarily replaced by decorations during the December holiday season.)

Hint 56: Spot the agriculture ("Agrifuture") sign from the train just past *"it's a small world"* after leaving Mickey's Toontown station. Above the peach stem in the sign, the top three grapes in the bunch of grapes come together to form a classic Mickey.

Frontierland

- Mark Twain Riverboat/ Sailing Ship Columbia

Hint 57: While boating the Rivers of America, look out for three boulders in the water that form a classic Mickey. These boulders are on the right side of your vessel near the shore of Tom Sawyer Island and across the river from an Indian scene.

Hint 58: Study the metal grillwork between the smokestacks and high above the *Mark Twain*'s prow for a sideways classic Mickey.

Hint 59: To the right of the entrance for the *Mark Twain Riverboat* is a "Shipping Office." A painting advertising river excursions on the *Mark Twain* hangs on an "office" wall. In the painting, Mickey Mouse is one of the passengers on the lowest deck.

- Big Thunder Mountain Railroad

Hint 60: As you start to climb the second hill, look to your left, near the bottom of the hill, for three gears that form a large, upside-down classic Mickey.

Hint 61: On your right as you exit, the highest three green lobes in the cactus garden form an oval classic Mickey. At times, other collections of cactus lobes may also form Mickeys.

- Tom Sawyer Island

Hint 62: As you exit the *Raft* onto the island, turn left and look above the first cavern entrance you encounter. A classic Mickey depression is in the rock over the entrance.

Hint 63: Stroll back to the heaps of coins in the *Pirate's Lair* play area. At the right rear of the coin heaps, look in front of the hanging blue pirate tarp for a wood plank that holds the treasure in place. Three coins that peek out from under the wood plank form a classic Hidden Mickey.

Tomorrowland

- Near Finding Nemo Submarine Voyage & the Monorail exit

Hint 64: From the *Disneyland Monorail* loading area or exit in Tomorrowland, you can often spot a classic Mickey made of coiled rope lying near the end of the *Finding Nemo Submarine Voyage* dock.

Hint 65: A classic Mickey impression is in the rock wall about one foot off the floor and between two separated handrails.

- Finding Nemo: Marine Observation Outpost

Hint 66: Look for the lockers on the left front wall inside the Marine Observation Outpost. You can spot Sorcerer Mickey inside locker No. 105. He's on the clothing that's under a pair of sunglasses.

- Innoventions

Hint 67: At times, a classic Mickey made of bubbles floats across the lower third of the large blue globe.

Hint 68: Under a glass pane in the outer row, directly in front of the middle of the globe, small blue beads stuck together form a classic Mickey. It's under the lower middle of the pane as you face the globe.

Hint 69: Another classic Mickey made of three beads stuck together hides under the second glass pane from the left wall in the second row of panes from the outside. This Mickey is under the lower third of the pane as you face the globe.

Hint 70: A shadow of Mickey runs across the large window near the front door, just outside the *Dream Home*.

Hint 71: In the large window with the Mickey shadow, a Mickey balloon is at the lower border of the collection of balloons, on the right side.

Hint 72: Classic Mickeys are in the middle of the railings just outside and inside the front door.

Hint 73: Classic Mickeys are among the circles in the main hallway carpet outside the bedrooms and leading toward the kitchen.

Hint 74: Side-profile Mickey-shaped bookends support the books on a middle shelf. Nearby on the same shelf is a small picture of Mickey kicking a soccer ball.

Hint 75: On a wall mural inside *Innoventions* but just outside the *Dream Home*, several classic Mickeys are formed by grapes at the lower part of vertical vines.

Hint 76: A small black classic Mickey hides in the lower part of a painting on a wall of the *ASIMO* stage.

Hint 77: On the *ASIMO* show stage, a Mickey doll sits on the desk next to the computer monitor.

Hint 78: When the lady talks to her husband over the videophone, you can see a side view of Mickey on the wall behind the husband.

Hint 79: Among items in the Entertainment section of the rotating wall murals outdoors is a black classic Mickey on a video monitor. In another mural, a large classic Mickey is on a blue wall, partially hidden behind a red monitor screen.

Hint 80: Also on the outside rotating murals, find a globe on a pedestal. Goofy's long nose pokes out from the eastern side of the land mass at the top. He's looking to the right.

- Autopia

Hint 81: A black classic Mickey hides in the upper right corner of the car license plates.

Fantasyland

- Mickey and the Magical Map Show

Hint 82: On the right upper corner of the decorative archway above the stage, three yellow circles form an upside-down classic Hidden Mickey.

Hint 83: A gold classic Mickey made of circles hides in the middle of a stained-glass window at the far left side of the stage set. This Hidden Mickey is best viewed from close to the stage.

Hint 84: During the show, Mickey interacts with an elusive black splotch. At one point, just for a second, the round splotch morphs into a classic Mickey!

Hint 85: During the "Under the Sea" segment of the show, a three-bubble classic Mickey floats up the rear screen.

Hint 86: When the stage map opens up during the "Under the Sea" segment of the show, some blue classic Hidden Mickey bubbles are inside larger bubbles on the rear screen.

- Fantasy Faire

Hint 87: Locate Clopin's Music Box for some interesting images. (To refresh, Clopin is the leader of the gypsies in the Disney movie *The Hunchback of Notre Dame*.) Look to the far left inside the Music Box to spot a tiny classic Mickey at the top of the second window from the left.

Hint 88: Many Disney characters are mixed in the crowd of people inside Clopin's Music Box, including Flynn Rider, Snow White, Doc, Sleepy, Peter Pan, Mr. Smee, Maurice, Belle, the Beast in human form, Gaston, a man from Gaston's tavern, Tony (from *Lady and the Tramp*), Geppetto, and the evil coachman who takes Pinocchio to Pleasure Island.

Critter Country

- *Splash Mountain*

Hint 89: A tiny classic Mickey is formed of indentations in a protruding knot on a post at the beginning of the outside standby entrance queue. Mickey is on the post just below the *Splash Mountain* Warning sign. You can also spot this Mickey as you exit *Haunted Mansion*.

Hint 90: As you enter the inside part of the entrance queue, look along the left side for a three-gear classic Mickey.

Hint 91: At the top of the last big climb, just before the big drop, three rocks stuck in the ceiling form a sideways classic Mickey, facing left.

Hint 92: Near the end of the ride, after the big drop, you can spot a framed photo of Mickey Mouse (riding in a *Splash Mountain* log) on the upper wall, to the left of your log. (Note: This image may come and go.)

Afternoon Parade

- *Grand Marshal automobile*

Hint 93: On this attractive replica of an antique touring car, classic Mickeys adorn the tires, the front bumper, the hood ornament, nuts at the side of the front windshield, the tread on the spare tire on the rear of the car, and the brackets holding the spare tire in place.

Adventureland

- *Tarzan's Treehouse*

Hint 94: Look for a trunk on the floor near the ship's wheel. The gold metal plate where the trunk's keyhole is located includes a classic Mickey made of round metal pieces. The keyhole is inside the classic Mickey's round "head."

Hint 95: Behind the ship's wheel, the far right curtain knobs at the right rear of the room form a classic Mickey. The curtain knobs directly to the left resemble a classic Mickey as well.

Hint 96: Pots that resemble Mrs. Potts and Chip from the *Beauty and the Beast* movie sit alongside the trail in the children's play area near the end.

- Indiana Jones Adventure Outpost

Hint 97: Inside the Indiana Jones Adventure Outpost shop, a classic Hidden Mickey is traced in the middle of an archeological pan sifter stuck high on the left wall.

- Enchanted Tiki Room

Hint 98: Four shields hang over the *Enchanted Tiki Room* exit. A classic Mickey with two smiley faces for "ears" hides near the bottom of the left shield.

Tomorrowland

- "Captain EO"

Hint 99: In the movie, the three lower thrusters on the back of Captain EO's spaceship form a classic Hidden Mickey.

Critter Country

- The Many Adventures of Winnie the Pooh

Hint 100: The back and lower legs of the "Heffabee" on top of each ride vehicle form an upside-down classic Mickey.

Hint 101: In the first part of the entrance tunnel, a small classic Hidden Mickey hides on the bark of a round tree trunk that you reach just before you get to the wall covered with colorful leaves. Mickey's to the right of your vehicle, at about eye level.

Hint 102: In the scene to the left of your vehicle where Winnie the Pooh is sleeping and begins to float in the air, you can spot Mickey ears on the upper shelf of a desk to the far side of Pooh, in the corner of the room.

Hint 103: As you leave the Heffalump and Woozle room, turn around in your vehicle and look up behind you to see Max the buck, Buff the buffalo, and Melvin the moose hanging on the wall above you. (These three animals pay homage to the original attraction in this location—*The Country Bear Playhouse*.)

Hint 104: Near the end of the ride, there is a Heffalump collage on your right. Look in the bottom right-hand corner to spot an upside-down classic Mickey.

- Briar Patch store

Hint 105: A classic Mickey made from heads of lettuce sits on an upper shelf over the front window inside the Briar Patch store.

Frontierland

- Big Thunder Ranch

Hint 106: At the entrance/exit, a classic Mickey formed by holes in the wood is under the soap dispenser next to the hand-washing station.

Hint 107: Behind a fence to the left of the Ranch Cabin, you can see a huge pile of leaves and horseshoes. Three horseshoes at the upper right of the pile are positioned to resemble a classic Mickey.

Fantasyland

- Casey Jr. Circus Train

Hint 108: In the middle of the control panel at the front of the conductor's cabin, three round dials form a classic Mickey. You can spot this Mickey from the entrance area, so you can skip the ride if you want.

- Storybook Land Canal Boats

Hint 109: On the middle of one side of the vertical strut at the rear of the "Daisy" boat, an upside-down classic Mickey is made of round flowers—a yellow "head" and pink "ears."

Hint 110: On the rear side of the "Flora" boat, a small purple classic Mickey is hiding in the flower design.

Hint 111: A classic Mickey formed of purple berries hangs on a vine on the back of the pilot's seat on the "Snow White" boat. One of the bluebirds in the painting is eyeing those special berries.

Hint 112: On the "Wendy" boat, a classic Mickey in relief hides on the upper back of the rear post.

Hint 113: The pumpkin carriage on the upper road approaching Cinderella's village simulates an upside-down classic Mickey. The pumpkin is the "head" and the side wheels are the "ears."

Adventureland

- Jungle Cruise

Hint 114: Beneath the outside *Jungle Cruise* sign, a mask that resembles Donald Duck hangs just above the entrance.

Hint 115: Listen for chanting and dancing natives on the left side of your boat; some are blowing long curved horns. Behind and to the right of the hornblowers, an image of Mufasa from *The Lion King* decorates a brown shield that stands in front of a straw hut.

Hint 116: Along the left side of the boat, be alert for menacing natives with spears. The next to last isolated native of the group wears a Donald mask.

Fantasyland

- Pinocchio's Daring Journey

Hint 117: When your vehicle enters the Pleasure Island room, study the ground in front of the popcorn stand on your right. Some "spilled" popcorn forms a classic Hidden Mickey.

Hint 118: Look back at the left side window in the popcorn stand for an upside-down classic Mickey in the popcorn, about one-third the way up in the window.

Hint 119: Near the end of the ride a big case holds a model ship. The middle of the top frame of the case is decorated with a wooden classic Mickey.

- Snow White's Scary Adventures

Hint 120: A somewhat distorted three-quarter side-profile Mickey is formed by bushes in the mural directly in front of your ride vehicle at the loading area. Look at the right end of the row of green bushes just past the rocky hill and to the left of the blue stream. Mickey is looking to the right.

Hint 121: Early on in the ride, look for the green turtle climbing the stairs to the left of your ride vehicle. The large circle on the left side of the turtle's shell forms the "head" of a three-circle classic Mickey.

- Alice in Wonderland

Hint 122: When the cards are "painting the roses red," look on the ground under the tree to the left for a slightly distorted red classic Mickey. It's on a third-level ledge under the right hand with the paintbrush and just to the left of a green heart.

Mickey's Toontown

- Near the entrance

Hint 123: A white silhouette of Mickey's face and ears, seen from the front, adorns the "Order of Mouse" seal on the overhead bridge to the left of the "Welcome to Mickey's Toontown" sign.

- In and outside of Minnie's House

Hint 124: Inside *Minnie's House*, you'll see a row of books in the first room on the right side. Look for a pink book next to a book entitled "Little Mouse on the Prairie." The mark at the top of the pink book's spine is a classic Mickey combined with the medical symbol for "female." (Could the symbol be a Hidden Minnie?)

Hint 125: Inside the refrigerator in Minnie's kitchen, a bottle of cheese relish on the second shelf in the door has a red classic Mickey "brand mark" at the top of the label.

Hint 126: To the right of the large blue doors that lead backstage near *Minnie's House*, a small opening leads to a "Cast Members Only" entrance and exit. Walk into this opening and look left to spot a blue rock classic Mickey in the wall.

- Approaching, in, and exiting Mickey's House

Hint 127: The window in Mickey's green front door is a partial classic-Mickey shape.

Hint 128: The welcome mat at Mickey's front door is shaped like a classic Mickey.

Hint 129: As you enter the first room, stop by the green, glass-fronted bookcase. The top of the spine of the book "2001: A Mouse Odyssey" is decorated with two gold classic Mickeys.

Hint 130: In the same bookcase, find the orange book, "See You Next Squeak." At the bottom of the spine, the publisher's logo is a classic Mickey enclosed in a square.

Hint 131: At the left side of the first room, the bottom of the spine of the blue book entitled "My Fair Mouse" sports a classic Mickey.

Hint 132: Just as you enter the piano room, study the bookcase on the right side. The book "My Life with Walt" has a pink classic Mickey at the top of the spine.

Hint 133: In the same bookcase, locate the book "Pluto's Republic." To its immediate left, a thin green book has a yellow classic Mickey at the top of its spine.

Hint 134: Most of the holes in the paper for the player piano are classic Mickeys, but one of the holes is shaped like Donald Duck and another, like Goofy!

Hint 135: The weight for the metronome on top of the player piano is a classic Mickey.

Hint 136: In the room with Mickey's drums, a drum with legs on the lower shelf has knobs with Mickey ears along its rim.

Hint 137: Also in the room with Mickey's drums, Mickey's gloves are on the hour and minute hands of a cuckoo clock on the wall.

Hint 138: There is a mirror on the right side inside Mickey's Movie Barn. Stare at it and wait awhile. Mickey Mouse's head will appear.

Hint 139: On your left as you continue walking, a paintbrush on the top right of Donald Duck's wooden workbench has pink paint splotches that form an upside-down classic Mickey.

Hint 140: Also in Mickey's Movie Barn (and before you meet Mickey Mouse in person), a classic Mickey appears around the countdown numbers on the screen before the film starts.

Hint 141: Mickey's red car sits outside his house in his driveway. The car's hubcaps and spare tire sport white classic Mickeys.

Hint 142: Outside the exit from *Mickey's House*, classic Mickeys hide in the decorative ironwork on a lamp sitting on a short post.

- Gadget's Go Coaster

Hint 143: The following three classic Mickeys aren't perfectly proportional, but they seem purposeful:
 - The first is at the first turn to the left in the entrance queue.
 - The second is across from a bonsai tree and before the last right turn.
 - The third is a somewhat distorted classic Mickey, facing sideways, at the end of the wall on the left and about 20 feet before the boarding area.

Hint 144: Inside the loading area, turn around and locate the only blueprint on the rear wall. A partial drawing of Mickey Mouse is on the right side of the blueprint. Under Mickey are the words "DOG & PONY FOR MICKEY AT 4 PM."

- Clarabelle's Frozen Yogurt

Hint 145: A shutter is pulled down when Clarabelle's Frozen Yogurt closes for business. A white classic Mickey marking is on the left side of the shutter.

- Toontown Post Office

Hint 146: At the Post Office, Mickey is on the postage stamp on the letter above the entrance. You'll also find a side profile of Mickey (along with five other decorative characters) inside the Post Office on the wall-mounted mailboxes.

- Toontown Fire Department

Hint 147: When you ring the doorbell at the Fire Department, move back quickly to spot the Dalmatian puppy who looks out of an upper middle window for a few seconds. A sideways classic Mickey made of black spots is on his upper forehead.

- Fireworks Factory

Hint 148: Face the Fireworks Factory and find a small, pink firework cone poking out from the right wall. It's one of the lower fireworks, and it has a small, blue classic Mickey painted halfway up its cone.

Fantasyland

- "it's a small world"

Hint 149: Three circular control towers topped by umbrellas overlook the entrance queue. The center tower is larger than the other two, so together they form a classic Mickey.

Hint 150: Disney characters appear alongside your tour boat. Look for Alice in Wonderland, Cinderella, Pinocchio, Ariel, Nemo, Woody and Jessie, Lilo and Stitch, and others.

Hint 151: Early in your boat ride look for a boy standing in a hot air balloon with a toy bear holding on to the ropes to the boy's right. The bear's head and ears cast a classic Hidden Mickey shadow on the balloon.

Hint 152: In the last room of the ride, shadows from a set of small balloons that move up and down form classic Mickeys at times to the left of your boat.

- King Arthur Carrousel

Hint 153: Find the white horse, Jingles. Classic Mickeys made of gemstones are on the front and back of the horse. These classic Mickeys aren't perfectly proportioned and the "ears" and "head" don't touch, but they seem purposeful. (Jingles is also adorned with images from the *Mary Poppins* movie.)

- The Mad Hatter

Hint 154: Every few minutes, a faint image of the Cheshire Cat appears in the mirror above the store's check-out area.

Hint 155: A Mickey hat with ears hides at one corner of each of two outdoor signs for the shop.

- Castle Heraldry Shoppe

Hint 156: Near the Castle Heraldry Shoppe, a classic Mickey is in the bottom center of the painted scroll trim at the edges of an outdoor mailbox. Also look for the classic Mickeys wearing "Mickey's Sorcerer's Hat." They're repeated at the end of some of the branches in the scrollwork at the top and bottom.

Tomorrowland

- Redd Rockett's Pizza Port

Hint 157: On a wall inside the restaurant, groups of circles decorate a poster entitled "Adventure Thru Inner Space." The circles in the middle right of the poster approximate a classic Mickey.

- The Star Trader

Hint 158: Classic Mickey holes are in some of the shop's upright merchandise display poles.

Hint 159: Some merchandise bins have classic Mickey feet and classic Mickey holes encircling the top rim.

- Little Green Men Store Command

Hint 160: A green side profile of Mickey Mouse hides on a planet at the right upper edge of the sign for this store near *Buzz Lightyear Astro Blasters*.

- Astro Orbitor

Hint 161: The moving spheres above the *Astro Orbitor* occasionally form classic Mickeys.

Frontierland

- Entrance walkway from the central hub

Hint 162: A cannon sits to the right, just past the Frontierland sign on the entrance walkway from the central hub. In the tongue behind the cannon is a classic Mickey, formed by a hole and two bolts.

- Frontierland Shootin' Exposition

Hint 163: In front of the "Nancy's Dan" tombstone, three lobes of a cactus resemble a classic Mickey.

- Pioneer Mercantile shop

Hint 164: On the walls inside the gift shop, white river rocks at the lower center of some of the lamp covers (the ones with bears) form classic Mickeys.

Hint 165: At the left rear of the store, light brown gourds hang high on a pole at the left side of a cashier's counter. They are usually arranged to resemble a classic Mickey.

- Rancho del Zocalo Restaurante

Hint 166: Halfway up a wooden support post near the corner of a wall behind a condiment and napkin cart, you can spot a classic Mickey depression in the wood. You'll see it best by looking back in from the exit with the gate on the restaurant's right side (as you approach the restaurant from the main Frontierland walkway).

- River Belle Terrace restaurant

Hint 167: A classic Mickey cutout decorates the back of a child's highchair.

Hint 168: A small white upside-down classic Hidden Mickey is repeated in the wallpaper inside the River Belle Terrace. The Mickey image is hiding among flowers and near a white bird perched on the right side of a hanging basket.

Main Street, U.S.A.

- Plaza Inn restaurant

Hint 169: To the right of the main entrance (as you enter), a framed painting of a floral arrangement includes an upside-down classic Mickey formed of roses.

- Photo Supply Company

Hint 170: On the middle of a high shelf behind the "Photo Preview" counter, a lens and two adjoining circles form a classic Mickey on the front of a camera.

- Silhouette Studio

Hint 171: In the front display window of the Silhouette Studio, the fancy frames on some of the displays include classic Mickeys. (These frames come and go, but a frame with classic Mickeys is almost always on display.)

- Fruit cart

Hint 172: A green classic Mickey hides on an axle under a fruit cart that is usually positioned midway along Main Street near the Disney Clothiers shop.

- In and near Main Street Cinema

Hint 173: Inside Main Street Cinema, some of the recessed lights on the sides of the step risers are shaped like classic Mickeys.

67

Hint 174: Outside, near Main Street Cinema, a "Casting Agency" sign on a door includes two classic Mickeys in the design, one at the top and one at the bottom.

- Main Street Magic Shop

Hint 175: Along the front counter inside the Magic Shop a white rope on a display shelf is coiled into a classic Mickey shape.

Hint 176: Look up! Playing cards are stuck on the ceiling and a black classic Mickey is in the center of the Ace of Clubs.

Hint 177: In an outside display window to the left of the Magic Shop's entrance, the ace on an Ace of Clubs playing card resembles a classic Mickey instead of a club.

- Penny Arcade

Hint 178: At the entrance, a small classic Mickey hides between the play buttons on a game machine called "Pinocchio, Make Him Dance."

- Gibson Girl Ice Cream Parlor

Hint 179: The words "Ice Cream Floats" are on an outside window to the right. A pink classic Mickey is midway up the right leg of the letter "A" in the word "Floats."

Hint 180: A bejeweled lamp hangs from the ceiling at the rear of the parlor. Along the lower part of the lamp, jewels are positioned to form classic Mickeys.

- Emporium store

Hint 181: Classic Mickeys hide at the top of ornate wire-framed bookstands in some of the store's outside display windows.

Hint 182: Walk into the store through the entrance facing Main Street. (It's at the end of the store closest to City Hall.) Look behind the cashier's counter to your right as you enter the store and search the wall for a still-life painting with flowers. A distorted but recognizable image of Sorcerer Mickey is on a blue globe, which sits on a small table in the painting.

Hint 183: Check out a room with toys at the end of the store closest to Carnation Café. A toy train makes a circuit on a track above you along the walls. Stand near the small water tower at one corner of the room. Every third or so trip around the track, the train stops in front of the water tower, and a classic Hidden Mickey lights up at the upper right side of the tower. You can also usually spot the faint Hidden Mickey image when it's not lit up.

- above The Mad Hatter

Hint 184: To the left of the Opera House, Disney sculptor Blaine Gibson is honored in one of the middle second-floor windows above The Mad Hatter. At the upper part of the window, under the words "The Busy Hands," two hands hold a blue carving. A classic Hidden Mickey forms the right end of the carving.

- Disneyland Railroad: Main Street Station

Hint 185: Classic Mickey-shaped holes are drilled into metal brackets behind the conductor's cabin on top of several of the tender tanks, for example, "Fred Gurley's" Engine No. 3 and "Ward Kimball's" Engine No. 5. You can spot these classic Mickeys from the side waiting queue or from inside the first car.

69

Frontierland

- *Fantasmic!*

Hint 186: During the *Fantasmic!* show, a classic Mickey appears on the water screen, outlined by white foam. You can spot it just before the scene with Mickey and the whirlpool.

Fireworks show

Hint 187: Disneyland's fireworks show often features a cluster of three exploding shells that form a classic Mickey.

Entrance Plaza between the theme parks

Hint 188: Some of the engraved personalized brick plaques at your feet along the entrance plaza feature a bell design. The bell ringer is a classic Mickey. (You'll also find decorative Mickey images on these plaques.)

Hint 189: Take a look at the directional signpoles. You'll find classic Mickey indentations on the bottoms of some of them, while the tops of the poles sport Mickey ears.

Disney California Adventure Scavenger Hunt

• •

★ Arrive at the entrance turnstiles (with your admission ticket) 45 minutes before the opening time for early entry (if you're eligible) or 45 minutes before the official opening time if you're not or if it's a non-early entry day.

★ Walk down to the end of Buena Vista Street and turn right. Get yourself a FASTPASS for *Soarin' Over California*.

★ Pass by "a bug's land" on your way to Cars Land. Line up for **Radiator Springs Racers**.

Clue 1: Take note of some cactuses along the standby entrance queue.
3 points

Clue 2: Look for a Hidden Mickey inside the Stanley's Cap 'n' Tap area of the standby entrance queue.
3 points

Clue 3: On the ride, if you go through Ramone's Body Art shop, keep your eyes peeled for Mickey on a wall-mounted electrical box.
5 points

Clue 4: On the ride, if you go through Luigi's tire shop, spot Mickey on a red toolbox.
5 points

Clue 5: While in the tire shop, watch behind Luigi for Hidden Mickeys.
5 points

★ Go to the FASTPASS distribution area near the entrance to *Grizzly River Run* to get a FASTPASS for the evening *World of Color* show.

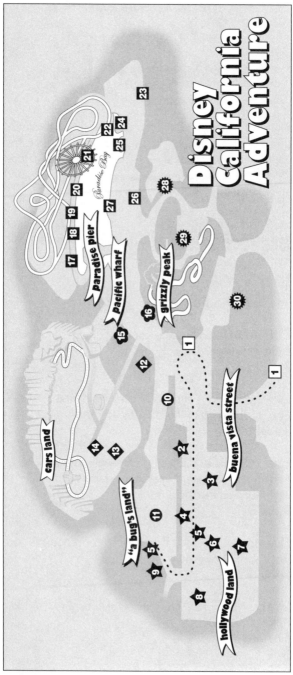

buena vista street

1 Red Car Trolley • • • •

★ hollywood land

2 Disney Junior — Live on Stage!
3 Muppet*Vision 3D
4 **Disney Animation:**
 Sorcerer's Workshop
 Character Close-Up
 Animation Academy
 Turtle Talk with Crush
5 Red Car Trolley
6 The Hollywood Backlot Stage
7 Monsters, Inc.
 Mike & Sulley to the Rescue!
8 Disney's Aladdin —
 A Musical Spectacular
9 The Twilight Zone Tower of Terror™

● "a bug's land"

10 It's Tough to be a Bug!
11 **Flik's Fun Fair:**
 Tuck and Roll's Drive 'Em Buggies
 Francis' Ladybug Boogie
 Flik's Flyers
 Princess Dot Puddle Park
 Heimlich's Chew Chew Train

◆ cars land

12 Mater's Junkyard Jamboree
13 Luigi's Festival of the Dance (coming 2016)
14 Radiator Springs Racers

❦ pacific wharf

15 The Bakery Tour
16 Walt Disney Imagineering
 Blue Sky Cellar

■ paradise pier

17 California Screamin'
18 King Triton's Carousel
19 Toy Story Midway Mania!
20 Games of the Boardwalk
21 Mickey's Fun Wheel
22 Silly Symphony Swings
23 Goofy's Sky School
24 Jumpin' Jellyfish
25 Golden Zephyr
26 The Little Mermaid –
 Ariel's Undersea Adventure
27 World of Color

✹ grizzly peak

28 Redwood Creek Challenge Trail
29 Grizzly River Run
30 Soarin' Over California

73

★ Walk to Paradise Pier, pass by Ariel's Grotto restaurant, and line up for **Toy Story Midway Mania!**

Clue 6: Along the entrance queue, search for a tiny Hidden Mickey on a poster.
4 points

Clue 7: Spot a classic Mickey at the loading dock.
2 points

Clue 8: On an interactive screen as you ride, look behind the target balloons in front of the volcano for a classic Mickey.
5 points

Clue 9: On another screen, watch the white plates for a classic Mickey image.
3 points

Clue 10: Find Mickey after you exit your vehicle.
3 points

Clue 11: After you exit *Toy Story Midway Mania!*, search for Mickey **on the promenade**.
4 points

★ Walk past *Mickey's Fun Wheel* to **Goofy's Sky School**.

Clue 12: As you approach *Goofy's Sky School*, admire a sign for a Hidden Mickey.
2 points

Clue 13: In the standby entrance queue, study two bulletin boards for two subtle Hidden Mickeys.
10 points for finding both

Clue 14: As you exit the ride vehicle, locate Mickey on a tool.
3 points

★ Ride **Soarin' Over California** at your FAST-PASS time.

Clue 15: Pay attention to the pre-show video for Mickey ears.
2 points

Clue 16: Also in the pre-show video, find some clothing characters.
4 points for spotting two Hidden Characters

Clue 17: While on the ride, look left for a Mickey balloon.
4 points

Clue 18: Now quickly look right for a Mickey shadow on the golf course.
4 points

Clue 19: Watch the ball hurtling toward you.
5 points

Clue 20: Search the sky over the castle.
3 points

Clue 21: Across from *Soarin' Over California*, look around for Mickey.
3 points

★ Now walk to *California Screamin'* in Paradise Pier and get a FASTPASS to ride later

★ In Cars Land, check out the entrance queue for **Luigi's Festival of the Dance** and earn some bonus points if these Hidden Mickeys are still there. (Luigi's was undergoing rehab when this guide went to press.)

Clue 22: Look for a tiny Lightning McQueen with Mickey ears.
5 bonus points

Clue 23: Find a drawing of a small red car with a Mickey-shaped headlight.
4 bonus points

Clue 24: Locate a small red car with Mickey ears and a black nose.
4 bonus points

75

★ Enter the queue for **Mater's Junkyard Jamboree**.

Clue 25: Search above you for a classic Mickey.
4 points

Clue 26: While in the queue, glance around the ride surface area for a Hidden Mickey, then enjoy the attraction if you wish. Or exit without riding to search for the next Hidden Mickey.
3 points

★ Mosey over to **"a bug's land."**

Clue 27: As you wander through "a bug's land," stay alert for a spoon in a drawing. Who is holding the spoon?
2 points

★ Enjoy a ride on **Heimlich's Chew Chew Train**.

Clue 28: Watch for Mickey on the wall.
4 points

Clue 29: After the train ride, walk around *Flik's Fun Fair* and glance below your feet.
2 points

Clue 30: Search for Mickey on a snack stand in "a bug's land."
3 points

★ Go to **Monsters, Inc. Mike & Sulley to the Rescue!** and line up.

Clue 31: Study the inside queue walls for a Hidden Mickey.
3 points

Clue 32: Watch the pre-show video monitor in the queue for a Hidden Mickey.
3 points

Clue 33: Before you board your vehicle, spot those headlights again!
2 points

Clue 34: At the beginning of the ride, search the sky-line for a tiny Hidden Mickey.
5 points

Clue 35: Don't miss the moving Mickey shadow on a wall along the ride!
5 points

Clue 36: Admire the color-changing Randall (the multi-legged lizard-shaped monster)!
5 bonus points

Clue 37: On the ride, look for a Hidden Mickey on Sulley.
4 points

Clue 38: Stay alert for Mickey near a monitor screen.
3 points

★ Stop by **Muppet∗Vision 3D**.

Clue 39: Watch for a Hidden Mickey in the pre-show.
3 points

Clue 40: Try to spot Mickey balloons during the show.
3 points

Clue 41: Study the license plate on the fire truck for a Hidden Surprise.
4 points

★ At your FASTPASS time, walk to **California Screamin'** and ride if you're brave enough!

Clue 42: While you're screamin', stay alert for a classic Mickey below you on the ground.
4 points

Clue 43: Find Mickey on a sign along the exit.
2 points

★ After settling your nerves, stroll to *Tower of Terror* to get a FASTPASS.

★ Consider lunch at the restaurant of your choice, or try one of the counter-service eateries such as Flo's V8 Café, Pacific Wharf Café, Cocina Cucamonga Mexican Grill, or Paradise Garden Grill.

★ While at lunch, check your Times Guide for the next show in Hyperion Theater (the show as we go to press is *Disney's Aladdin—A Musical Spectacular*) and check for convenient show times for *Disney Junior—Live on Stage!* and the *Five & Dime* show in Carthay Circle.

★ At the time you've chosen, see the show at **Hyperion Theater**.

Clue 44: Look around for a Hidden Mickey inside the theater, near the seats.
3 points

★ At a convenient time, visit **Disney Junior—Live on Stage!**

Clue 45: Watch for Mickey images during the show.
3 points for spotting two or more

★ Amble over to Carthay Circle for the **Five & Dime** show you selected.

Clue 46: Study the car in the show.
3 points

★ Enter Hollywood Land, then stand outside the **Disney Animation Building**.

Clue 47: Look up for a Hidden Mickey on a pole.
3 points

Clue 48: Now search for Mickey on the outside wall of the Animation Building.
2 points total for one or more

Clue 49: Search for a classic Hidden Mickey high on a shelf inside the **Animation Academy**.
3 points

Clue 50: Study the left side of the stage for a classic Mickey.
5 points

★ Walk through the **Sorcerer's Workshop**.

Clue 51: Locate two Hidden Mickeys on the wall.
4 points for spotting both

Clue 52: Spot Hidden Mickeys along the Animation Building's exit hall.
3 points total for one or more

Clue 53: Find two Hidden Mickeys in the wall posters outside.
4 points for spotting both

Clue 54: Study the pictures in the glass nearby for a classic Mickey.
3 points

Clue 55: Search a display window nearby for a Hidden Mickey.
3 points

Clue 56: Look for Mickey on the ceiling inside the **Off the Page** store.
4 points

★ Cross the street to **Schmoozies**.

Clues 57, 58, and 59: Check out the outside walls for Hidden Mickeys.
5 points total for finding three Hidden Mickeys

Clue 60: Spot Minnie Mouse behind the order windows!
5 points

★ Walk to "a bug's land." Watch **It's Tough to be a Bug!**

Clue 61: After the show, exit near the front of the theater and look up for a classic Mickey.
5 points

★ Mosey toward Paradise Pier and then turn right to the **Redwood Creek Challenge Trail**.

Clue 62: Tarry at the large trail map just inside the entrance and spot three classic Mickeys.
5 points for finding all three

Clue 63: Mickey is near a cave inside the trail area.
3 points

Clue 64: Find a Mickey reference in the Mt. Whitney Lookout.
5 points

★ Check out the **Rushin' River Outfitters** shop near *Grizzly River Run*.

Clue 65: Search for Hidden Mickeys on the merchandise inside the shop.
3 points

★ Walk past the entrance to *Grizzly River Run* to the **fence overlooking the raft stream**.

Clue 66: Investigate the area near the fence for a Hidden Mickey.
4 points

★ Stroll to Paradise Pier and enjoy **The Little Mermaid ~ Ariel's Undersea Adventure**.

Clue 67: Look for Mickey along the outside entrance queue.
2 points

Clue 68: Can you see Mickey in the lights?
2 points

Clue 69: Don't miss the Hidden Mickey on the loading dock mural!
4 points

Clue 70: As you enter the room where the "Under the Sea" song is playing, study the purple coral for a classic Mickey.
5 points

80

Clue 71: Watch the spinning purple octopus for a Hidden Mickey.
4 points

Clue 72: Two Hidden Images are near the singing Ariel. Stare below her for the first one: a coral Hidden Mickey.
5 points

Clue 73: Now look quickly to your right across from Ariel for a Hidden Mr. Limpet!
5 points

Clue 74: Check out the frogs along the ride!
4 points for one or more

Clue 75: Now look behind the frogs for a Hidden Mickey in the water.
4 points

★ During your FASTPASS window, enjoy **_The Twilight Zone Tower of Terror™_**.

Clues 76 and 77: Spot a Mickey doll during the pre-show and on the ride.
3 points for each sighting; 6 points total

Clue 78: In the boiler room before the elevator ride, look around for Mickey on a gauge.
3 points

Clue 79: Line up in front of the lower leftmost elevator and admire Mickey.
5 points

Clue 80: If you approach the far right elevator on the lower level, look around for a Mickey lock.
3 points

Clue 81: If you're near the far left elevator on the upper level, spot Mickey on the wall.
3 points

Clue 82: Find Mickey in displays along the exit after the ride.
3 points

Clue 83: Say goodbye one last time to the little girl and her Mickey doll!
3 points

Clue 84: Outside the *Tower of Terror*, search for two Mickeys on a gate.
4 points for finding both

★ Check out **Walt Disney Imagineering Blue Sky Cellar** for some Hidden Mickeys.

Clue 85: Study the sign outside.
4 points

Clue 86: Now admire Mickey in the first mural inside.
4 points

Clue 87: Find a classic Mickey on a palette in the main room.
3 points

Clue 88: Search for a classic Mickey in a photo.
3 points

Clue 89: Outside *Blue Sky Cellar*, look for Mickey in Pinot Grigio grapes.
3 points

★ Walk to the left of **Cars Land**.

Clue 90: Make a detour into the **Radiator Springs Racers** FASTPASS queue and find a Hidden Mickey on the fence.
5 points

Clue 91: Look under the sign at the entrance to Cars Land for a Hidden Mickey.
4 points

Clue 92: Gaze inside the office of the **Cozy Cone Motel** for a Hidden *Cars* movie character and a Hidden Mickey.
5 points for both

82

Clue 93: Mater poses at times for photos near the motel. Study him for a Hidden Mickey.
3 points

Clue 94: Outside the **Radiator Springs Curios Store**, check around for a classic Hidden Mickey.
5 points

Clue 95: Find a classic Mickey on the wall inside Radiator Springs Curios Store.
2 points

Clue 96: Glance up for Mickey inside the store.
2 points

★ Spend some time studying the six colorful car hoods in the outside display windows of **Ramone's House of Body Art**.

Clues 97 to 102: Mickey hides somewhere on each car hood! Start with the rightmost display window.
30 points for finding all six

Clue 103: Admire the purple car hood behind the front counter inside Ramone's and try to find Mickey.
5 points

Clue 104: Now spot Mickey on pillars inside the store.
2 points

Clue 105: Look around for Mickey images on merchandise boxes.
4 points for one or more

Clue 106: Outside Ramone's House of Body Art, search for Mickey near a pole.
5 points

★ Go to Paradise Pier and stop by the **Seaside Souvenirs** shop near *Jumpin' Jellyfish*.

Clue 107: Find Mickey on a wall inside the shop.
3 points

Clue 108: Now spot two references to Jules Verne in this shop!
4 points for both

★ Enter the **Sideshow Shirts** store, not far from *Mickey's Fun Wheel*.

Clue 109: Look around for a small Hidden Mickey near some nails.
4 points

Clue 110: Search for a Hidden Mickey on a wall inside the store.
4 points

★ Take a look inside the **Man Hat n' Beach** store.

Clue 111: Locate a Hidden Mickey on a merchandise stand.
3 points

★ Enter the **Point Mugu Tattoo** store.

Clue 112: Spot a Hidden Mickey on a wall.
3 points

★ Now stroll **along the promenade**.

Clue 113: Search the *Games of the Boardwalk* buildings for a Hidden Mickey.
3 points

Clue 114: Find Donald Duck on the promenade outside *King Triton's Carousel*.
3 points

★ Enter the **Treasures in Paradise** shop.

Clue 115: Find a Hidden Mickey on an animal inside the store.
2 points

Clue 116: Look for Mickey in a painting.

4 points

★ Check out the seating area of **Cove Bar**.

Clue 117: Admire the furniture for Hidden Mickeys.
2 points for one or more

★ Stroll inside **Ariel's Grotto** restaurant.

Clue 118: Head down the stairs to the right to locate Mickey.
3 points

★ Walk over to **The Bakery Tour** in nearby Pacific Wharf.

Clue 119: Look around and locate Mickey inside the entrance to the *Tour*.
2 points

★ Return to **Buena Vista Street** to find more Hidden Mickeys.

Clue 120: Look down along the entrance area in front of **Carthay Circle Restaurant** for a Hidden Mickey.
5 points

Clue 121: Inside **Clarabelle's Hand-Scooped Ice Cream Shop**, search for Mickey on a display bottle.
5 points

Clue 122: Find two Hidden Mickeys in a window of the **Julius Katz & Sons** store.
4 points for spotting both

Clue 123: Inside Julius Katz & Sons, search near a fan on a shelf for a Hidden Mickey.
4 points

Clue 124: Inside **Big Top Toys** store, locate a Hidden Mickey on a mural.
4 points

Clue 125: **Near Oswald's**, scan a blue advertisement on an outside wall for Mickey.
5 points

Clue 126: Spot a classic Mickey at the **Trolley Station** near the main park entrance.
3 points

★ Exit Disney California Adventure Park to the **main entrance plaza**.

Clue 127: Look over the trees in the entrance plaza for Hidden Mickeys.
3 points

Clue 128: Check out some ticket buildings for Hidden Mickeys.
2 points

★ Rest, relax, have some dinner, and plan on returning for the **World of Color** show in Paradise Bay.

Clue 129: Watch the nightly World of Color show to spot a Mickey balloon.
5 points

Now total your score.

Total Points for Disney California Adventure Park =

How'd You Do?

Up to 181 points – Bronze
182 to 361 points – Silver
362 points and over – Gold
453 points – Perfect Score

You may have done even better if you earned bonus points in Luigi's Festival of the Dance entrance queue or Monsters, Inc. Mike & Sulley to the Rescue!

**Caution:
Don't peek at this
section unless you
really want help!**

Cars Land

- Radiator Springs Racers

Hint 1: A classic Mickey made of three barrel cactuses sits on the ground along the right side of the standby entrance queue. It's just past a pole with a sign that says "Long Trip? One Sip and Watch Those Miles Melt Away."

Hint 2: Inside the Stanley's Cap 'n' Tap covered area along the standby entrance queue, a wedding photo of Stanley and Lizzie is on a wall. A classic Mickey is formed of circles above Lizzie's forehead in the middle of her veil.

Hint 3: On the ride, if you go through Ramone's Body Art shop, look back to your right in the second room of the shop to spot a classic Mickey made of circles on an electrical box. It's on the right rear wall just past the doors between the rooms of Ramone's shop.

Hint 4: On the ride, if you go through Luigi's tire shop, watch on your right for a red toolbox that sits behind a rack of tires. Three inner circles in a design on the side of the box form a classic Mickey.

Hint 5: Also in Luigi's tire shop, glance in the window behind Luigi to spot moving light images that include small classic Mickey shapes.

Paradise Pier

- Toy Story Midway Mania!

Hint 6: Along the inside part of the winding entrance queue, spots near a blue dinosaur's left eye and upper horn form a classic Mickey, tilted to the right. The dino, Trixie from *Toy Story*, is near the right lower corner of a poster labeled "Dino Darts."

Hint 7: On the wall at the loading area, a classic Mickey is formed by three picture frames with *Toy Story* characters.

Hint 8: Watch for the screen with target balloons in front of the volcano spewing lava. If you pop the middle 100-point balloon on the second tier, a faint classic Mickey appears on the rear surface in the lava behind the balloons.

Hint 9: Be alert for the screen with moving white plates. At one point, a large front plate aligns with smaller plates behind it to form a classic Mickey.

Hint 10: Along the exit walkway from the ride, a "Toy Story Midway" game sits on a rug in a display room to the left. On the left side of the game box, three ovals (containing pictures of Jessie, Rex, and Bullseye the horse) form a classic Mickey.

- On the promenade

Hint 11: Across from *Toy Story Midway Mania!*, Steamboat Willie Mickey is pictured on faux newspapers stacked at a drink stand.

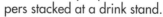

- *Goofy's Sky School*

Hint 12: As you walk toward *Goofy's Sky School*, look up at a sign for the attraction that shows Goofy flying a red plane. Three large holes in the sign form a sideways classic Mickey.

Hint 13: Along the standby entrance queue, check the walls for cork bulletin boards. On the first board, three round impressions in the cork form a classic Mickey. It's tilted to the right, and it's at the right lower side of the upside-down note that says, "Notice to Appear." A similar classic Hidden Mickey made of impressions is on the second bulletin board on another wall along the queue. This one is tilted to the left and is partially covered by the left side of a handwritten letter that says "Dear Teach." Look above the right upper corner of a note that reads "I Fix Planes!" to spot it.

Hint 14: As you exit the ride vehicle, look for a classic Mickey at the top of the handle of a wrench that's hanging on a wall at the far right of a tool rack.

Grizzly Peak

- *Soarin' Over California*

Hint 15: In the pre-show video, a man is asked to remove his Mickey Mouse ears.

Hint 16: Also in the pre-show, a boy sitting in his ride seat is wearing a shirt with a Grumpy logo and shorts sporting Mickey Mouse.

Hint 17: When you soar over the hills and spot a golf course, look immediately to your lower left and find a golf cart. The man standing on the other side of the cart is holding a blue Mickey balloon.

Hint 18: Look to the right side of the golf course. On the green grass, about halfway along the fairway, is a slightly distorted shadow classic Mickey formed by a cluster of three trees. The "ears" of the shadow Mickey touch the right side of the white cart path.

Hint 19: Look straight ahead and down to the golf course. Spot the man about to swing a golf club. When he strikes the golf ball, it will head directly toward you. Watch the ball's rotation to see the dark classic Mickey on the surface of the ball.

Hint 20: You complete your *Soarin'* ride over Disneyland. Watch the evening fireworks explode before you; the second burst forms a huge classic Mickey in the sky.

Hint 21: Across from *Soarin' Over California*, a side-profile white cloud Mickey floats on a red-and-white checkerboard background on a tower near the merchandise shop.

Cars Land

- *Luigi's Festival of the Dance*

Hint 22: Along the entrance queue, as you enter the second room inside, look for collages on the right wall. Behind glass, in the third collage from the right, a tiny red Lightning McQueen antenna topper has a Mickey hat with ears on its roof. This antenna topper is in the right middle part of the collage, below a white piece of paper on which someone has written, "# 121."

Hint 23: In the same room, the fourth glass-covered collage from the right has a red car with a sideways classic Mickey headlight. The car is above a sign for Buckingham Palace, in the right middle of the collage.

Hint 24: Along the entrance queue, at the rear of Luigi's office, a tiny red car with Mickey ears sits on the desk under a lamp.

- *Mater's Junkyard Jamboree*

Hint 25: Three hubcaps form a classic Mickey, tilted to the left, in the entrance

queue of *Mater's Junkyard Jamboree*. As you enter the covered area of the queue, they're above you at the far left corner near the ceiling.

Hint 26: Further along the queue, you can see three barrels inside the ride area that are positioned and proportioned to form a classic Mickey standing upright. A red barrel serves as the "head."

"a bug's land"

Hint 27: In "a bug's land," glance up as you walk toward a covered passageway themed as a cereal box. At the beginning of the passageway, Woody's hand is above you on the right, and he's holding a spoon filled with Cowboy Crunchies cereal.

- Heimlich's Chew Chew Train

Hint 28: Near the end of the ride, the train stops prior to re-entering the station. Three rocks in the shape of a classic Mickey are embedded in a wall to the right of the ride vehicle. If you are seated in row 4, the Hidden Mickey will be close by.

Hint 29: Outside in Flik's Fun Fair, you can often spot classic Hidden Mickeys in the pavement formed of flat round stones. Look near the various attractions in this area, especially *Heimlich's Chew Chew Train* and *Flik's Flyers*.

Hint 30: A classic Mickey made of cherries is on the front of a fruit drink stand, which is often located near *Heimlich's Chew Chew Train*.

Hollywood Land

- Monsters, Inc.
Mike & Sulley to the Rescue!

Hint 31: On the "Monstropolis Cab Co." wall poster, the taxicab headlights form an upside-down classic Mickey.

Hint 32: During the video loop on the queue monitors, a taxi appears with the words "Please Proceed" on the front bumper. The headlights of this vehicle are shaped like upside-down classic Mickeys.

Hint 33: The taxi with the upside-down headlight classic Mickeys is pictured on the side of your vehicle.

Hint 34: As your vehicle begins to move, look at the skyline behind a tall wall to your left. A tiny black classic Mickey is visible through holes along the top of the wall. Look along the skyline. You'll find this Mickey below the green "Downtown" sign and to the left of a tall vertical pipe behind the wall.

Hint 35: To the left of your ride vehicle, a side-profile shadow of the main mouse moves from left to right along the windows in the wall of the Harryhausen's restaurant scene. (Try to spot his moving shadow on the right wall, too!)

Hint 36: Watch for "Boo" on top of Randall's back. She pounds on Randall's head with a bat, causing his camouflage coloration to change continually. At one point, his body turns lime green (or sometimes yellow) with a blue (or purple) classic Mickey spot on his belly above a lower leg. (Note: This great image is visible only intermittently and not on every ride-through. Good luck!)

Hint 37: Sulley appears several times during the ride. A dark classic Mickey marking is on Sulley's left upper thigh the last time he appears (by the pink door).

Hint 38: Near the end of the ride, a classic Mickey is formed by dials and gauges on a control panel under the right monitor screen.

- Muppet*Vision 3D

Hint 39: Early in the pre-show on the monitors, check the screen for a test pattern with a classic Mickey shape.

Hint 40: Near the end of the movie, after

the cannon shoots holes in the theater, some of the observers outside are holding Mickey balloons.

Hint 41: Near the end of the movie, an image of Sleeping Beauty Castle (a Hidden Surprise) is on a license plate at the right lower corner of the fire truck Kermit is riding.

Paradise Pier

- California Screamin'

Hint 42: When you're upside down in the loop, look at the ground to your left for a classic Mickey cement footing at the base of one of the vertical support poles. You can also spot this Mickey if you look right as you ride through the little hills that cover the *Toy Story Midway Mania!* attraction building.

Hint 43: Classic Mickeys are atop the frames of the sample photos on the sign advertising the California ScreamCam. (Note: You can see this Hidden Mickey without riding the coaster.)

Hollywood Land

- Hyperion Theater

Hint 44: Classic Mickeys are at the top center of the frames over several of the doors inside the theater.

- Disney Junior—Live on Stage!

Hint 45: Classic Mickeys appear at times in the lighting and stage effects and on various stage props during the live show.

Buena Vista Street

- Five & Dime show

Hint 46: The tires on the *Five & Dime* show vehicle have classic Mickeys in the tread.

Hollywood Land

- Disney Animation Building

Hint 47: A small classic Mickey sits atop the flagpole over the front of the Animation Building.

Hint 48: Along the top of some outside windows and wall pillars, classic Mickey "hats" are in the tile design.

Hint 49: A drum set shaped like a classic Mickey sits on a shelf high above the stage inside the *Animation Academy*. You'll also find many decorative Mickey images on and around the stage.

Hint 50: Inside the *Animation Academy* theater, several subtle classic Hidden Mickeys are formed of impressions in the middle side of a clay vase sitting at the left side of the stage.

Hint 51: In the *Sorcerer's Workshop* area, Sorcerer Mickey is on the left wall toward the end of the room. He's encircled by classic Mickey bubbles. Nearby on the left wall, you'll find a classic Mickey intertwined with the middle of a treble clef.

Hint 52: In the mosaic lettering on the exit walls, large and small circles form many classic Mickeys.

Hint 53: Shadows of two people with Mickey ears decorate the bottoms of two posters on the wall outside; one poster is entitled "Turtle Talk with Crush" and the other "Character Close-up."

Hint 54: In the tall green glass wall outside, an upside-down classic Mickey made of specks of pixie dust floats above and to the left of the rightmost fairy godmother's pointed hat. The Hidden Mickey is about halfway up the right side of the glass wall.

- Off the Page shop

Hint 55: In an outside display window of the shop, the last of several Dalmatians

has an upside-down classic Mickey made of spots on its rear thigh.

Hint 56: On a drawing hanging from the ceiling in the middle of Off the Page, bubbles form a classic Mickey in front of the shadow of an alligator's front leg.

- Schmoozies

Hint 57: Face Schmoozies from the street, and then walk to the left side of the snack shop. There are two murals on the left wall. The one on the right has classic Mickeys formed by small round green and white pieces of colored glass.

Hint 58: Now face the shop from Hollywood Boulevard. A classic Mickey formed by three tan stones hides to the right of a knife tip and above a pink cup on the right side of the rightmost mural on the front of the shop.

Hint 59: Near the center of the mosaic mural closest to Fairfax Market, a red jewel with two button ears forms a classic Mickey. It's to the right of the word "EAT."

Hint 60: On the rear wall directly behind the front smoothie order windows, a Hidden Minnie Mouse decked out as the Statue of Liberty is in the middle and near the top of the wall mosaic.

"a bug's land"

- It's Tough to be a Bug!

Hint 61: As you exit the theater for *It's Tough to be a Bug!*, look for a classic Mickey as you walk toward the second set of exit doors, counting from the front of the theater. It's made of small round stalks and is hiding on the wall to the upper left.

Grizzly Peak

- Redwood Creek Challenge Trail

Hint 62: You'll find three classic Mickeys on the left side of the trail map. A group of three rocks in a stream forms a Hidden Mickey at the top left of the map. Three circles in the middle left form a classic Mickey in foam (look just to the left of the mouth of the left water slide). Lower down, three log seats in the Ahwahnee Camp Circle are arranged to create a classic Mickey.

Hint 63: At the rear of the trail area, three gray rocks embedded in the ground in front of Kenai's Spirit Cave form a classic Mickey.

Hint 64: Climb the stairs to the Mt. Whitney Lookout and check out the phonetic spelling alphabet (also known as the NATO phonetic alphabet and more accurately as the International Radiotelephony Spelling Alphabet) on a sheet of paper atop a table in the Lookout room. The word for "M" in the official phonetic spelling alphabet is "Mike." But this is Disney! So the word for "M" is—you guessed it—"Mickey"!

- Rushin' River Outfitters shop

Hint 65: On some of the stuffed grizzly bears, the rear pads on the bottoms of the paws are shaped like classic Mickeys.

- Near Grizzly River Run entrance

Hint 66: A classic Mickey made of rocks is embedded in the pavement under the right side of the fence, close to the "Grizzly Peak Airfield Recreation Area" cabin.

Paradise Pier

- The Little Mermaid ~
Ariel's Undersea Adventure

Hint 67: Classic Mickey circles hide in the design of the ironwork along the sides of the upper support for the entrance queue cover.

Hint 68: As you enter the queue inside the building, the globes in the chandeliers merge together from certain vantage points to form classic Mickeys.

Hint 69: A small classic Mickey is impressed in a large rock at the lower left corner of the loading dock mural, just above the green tile. You can spot this Hidden Mickey from the entrance queue and again as you pass by it on your right in your seashell vehicle.

Hint 70: Just before you enter the room where the song "Under the Sea" is playing, a collection of purple coral appears to your left above some starfish on a brown rock outcropping. A classic Mickey is formed by three holes on the upper part of the top round coral.

Hint 71: In the same room, three pink spots near the middle of the spinning purple octopus's head form a classic Mickey.

Hint 72: As you approach the singing Ariel, stare at the standing tubular coral stalks below her. In the middle of the group of corals, the round tops of three stalks form a classic Mickey tilted to the right.

Hint 73: Also in the "Under the Sea" song room, a blue Hidden Mr. Limpet (Don Knotts as a fish) wearing glasses is peeking out from the green seaweed. He's across from and just past the singing Ariel, and you have to look to your right to spot him. (Not a Hidden Mickey, but a cool Hidden Surprise!)

Hint 74: Toward the end of the ride, check the pond (to your right) for frogs with dark spots on their backs that form sideways classic Mickeys.

Hint 75: To the rear left of the boat with Ariel and Eric and behind the frogs and fish, three lily pads form a classic Mickey on the water.

Hollywood Land

- The Twilight Zone Tower of Terror™

Hint 76: In the pre-show video in the library, the little girl is holding a Mickey doll.

Hint 77: On the ride, the little girl appears again, still holding the Mickey doll in her right hand.

Hint 78: After you leave the library pre-show video room and soon after you enter the basement boiler room, check the right side of the aisle for a group of circular gauges. One gauge in the group has a black classic Mickey shape at the end of a needle pointing to the right. It's easier to see from the lower-level queue.

Hint 79: Above the lower loading area for the leftmost elevator, a classic Mickey made of three spotlights is projected on the ceiling grate.

Hint 80: A Mickey-shaped lock is attached to the fence that faces the rightmost elevator on the lower level.

Hint 81: Near the leftmost elevator on the upper level, gauges to the left of the elevator door form a Hidden Mickey. A larger gauge along the bottom forms the head and two smaller gauges, the "ears" of a classic Mickey tilted to the left.

Hint 82: Circles on the front of some of the cameras in displays along the exit form classic Mickeys. Among them is one on a camera in the leftmost display window under the ride-photo review monitors.

Others are on some of the cameras sitting on shelves behind the photo purchase counter.

Hint 83: As you leave the gift shop, you can wave goodbye to the girl and her Mickey doll from the *Tower of Terror* story. The two are at the exit in a photo on the wall to the left of the photo purchase counter.

Hint 84: Outside *The Twilight Zone Tower of Terror*, near the pathway to "a bug's land," look for a sign on a gate that says "California – On the Red Car Trolley." A postcard in the sign has two classic Mickeys, one on a Ferris wheel and another (an upside-down image) in the reflection of the Ferris wheel in the water.

Pacific Wharf

- *Walt Disney Imagineering Blue Sky Cellar*

Hint 85: On a sign outside, a tiny classic Mickey hides at the lower left in the swirling path of sparkles.

Hint 86: A cloud image of Sorcerer Mickey is at the lower left of the blue mural just inside the entrance.

Hint 87: A black classic Mickey lies on a paint palette in an Imagineering art display in the main room.

Hint 88: Stanley and Lizzie's wedding photo hangs on the left wall of the theater room. A classic Mickey is formed of circles above Lizzie's forehead in the middle of her veil.

Hint 89: Along an outside walkway behind *Blue Sky Cellar*, three grapes in a painting of white wine grapes form a classic Mickey on the left branch at the upper left of a group of Pinot Grigio grapes.

Cars Land

- Radiator Springs Racers FASTPASS queue

Hint 90: Before exploring Cars Land, step into the *Radiator Springs Racers* FASTPASS queue, which is to the left of the main walkway from Buena Vista Street and before you get to the entrance to "a bug's land." Walk to the fourth fencepost (from the queue's entrance) on the queue's right-hand fence railing and search the top of the post for a classic Hidden Mickey marking.

- Sign at Cars Land's entrance

Hint 91: There's a cactus bed in front of the large "Welcome to Cars Land" sign at Cars Land's entrance. On the right side of the group of cactuses, three cactuses next to ground lights for the sign form a classic Mickey.

- Cozy Cone Motel

Hint 92: Inside the Cozy Cone Motel office, Buzz Lightyear peeks out from under an orange cone on a shelf at the end of a counter. He can be spotted from a rear window of the office, which is locked and closed to guests. A Hidden Mickey figurine is on the lower shelf at the other end (the front) of the counter. (Note: At times, you may spot other Hidden Characters on these shelves.)

– Stars of Cars Greeting Area

Hint 93: The wing nut on Mater's engine air filter has Mickey ears.

- Radiator Springs Curios Store

Hint 94: On the far left lower wall of the front porch of Radiator Springs Curios Store, a classic Mickey is on the upper right outer edge of a yellow "Pump" sign. (Note: Sometimes this sign is partially hidden by furniture or other objects on the porch.)

Hint 95: Inside the store, on the wall to the right of the cashier, a yellow "Service" sign and two round red hubcaps form a classic Mickey.

Hint 96: Some groups of circles on the ceiling inside the store form classic Mickeys.

- Ramone's House of Body Art store

Hint 97: In the rightmost outside display window of Ramone's House of Body Art, a small white classic Mickey, tilted to the right, lies in a light yellow square area about halfway up the right side of the car hood.

Hint 98: In a nearby window, spot a car hood with orange and yellow "flames." A classic Mickey hides on the far right side of the hood under the rightmost blue vertical streak.

Hint 99: In the next window, a tiny white classic Hidden Mickey is at the middle bottom of a brown car hood with a pinstripe design. You have to look very low to see this one!

Hint 100: Moving to your left, another car hood hosts a faint white classic Mickey. It's on the right side, in the bottom red fringe of the second blue-and-red vertical design from the right.

Hint 101: In the second outside display window from the far left, a subtle white classic Mickey hides in the red flame in the lower middle of a bronze and white car hood. It's in a trough of the flame just to the right of midline. This Hidden Mickey is very hard to spot!

Hint 102: In the outside display window at the far left of the storefront, a white classic Mickey is in the lacy fabric at the lower middle of a car hood.

Hint 103: Inside the store, a faint white classic Mickey is on the right side of a purple car hood that stands behind the front sales counter. It's just above and to the far right of the word "Ramone's."

Hint 104: Classic Mickeys are part of the decorative pinstripe design on the support pillars inside Ramone's.

Hint 105: Subtle classic Mickeys are traced on a few paint-splattered boxes on the floor and on shelves inside the store.

- Near the Fire Department building

Hint 106: A sideways classic Mickey is high up on a power line that hangs on a telephone pole to the left of the statue of Stanley the car, near the Town of Radiator Springs Fire Department building.

Paradise Pier

- Seaside Souvenirs shop

Hint 107: Look for one or more Mickey balloons painted high on the walls behind merchandise shelves inside the shop.

Hint 108: Two brown Nautilus submarines are also painted behind the shelves. (Note: "Nautilus" is the submarine, commanded by Captain Nemo, in Jules Verne's novel *Twenty Thousand Leagues Under the Sea*.)

- Sideshow Shirts store

Hint 109: Toward the front of the store, find a painting of a man lying on a bed of nails. A small classic Mickey hides in the wood on the side of the bed.

Hint 110: A painting of a woman named Betty hangs on the rear wall of the store. A classic Mickey is etched in the wood on the middle of the right side of the picture frame.

- Man Hat n' Beach store

Hint 111: On a merchandise stand inside the store, a classic Mickey is on the back of an octopus's head.

- Point Mugu Tattoo store

Hint 112: On the rear wall near the ceiling, a classic Mickey hides on a sign between the words "Paradise" and "Pier."

- Along the promenade

Hint 113: White classic Mickey designs are under the high eaves of the *Games of the Boardwalk* building with the "Paradise Pier Amusements Co." sign.

Hint 114: A row of Donald Ducks is atop each of two large gazebo shelters next to the lake near *King Triton's Carousel*.

- Treasures in Paradise shop

Hint 115: A classic Mickey adorns the side (toward the bottom) of a lion's saddle in a store display.

Hint 116: In the "Azalea" painting of a lady behind a service counter, a classic Mickey is formed by circles in the area where the wide belt loops connect below her waist.

- Cove Bar

Hint 117: Classic Mickeys hide in the design of the chair backs in the seating area.

- Ariel's Grotto restaurant

Hint 118: Along the wall across from the bottom of the staircase inside the restaurant, white classic Mickey bubbles hide at the lower left of the display sign for "Ariel's Grotto Disney Princess Celebration."

Pacific Wharf

- The Bakery Tour

Hint 119: On a table in a corner of the first room, you'll see bread rolls. Sometimes they're shaped like Mickey; other times they're imprinted with him.

Buena Vista Street

- 1901 Lounge

Hint 120: A tiny white classic Hidden Mickey hides in the white tile in front of the entrance door to the 1901 Lounge next to the entrance to Carthay Circle Restaurant.

- Clarabelle's Hand-Scooped Ice Cream Shop

Hint 121: Along a rear wall inside the shop, the cows on the Clarabelle's Dairy Milk bottles displayed behind the counter have classic Mickey spots on their sides.

- Julius Katz & Sons store

Hint 122: In an outside display window of the store, a classic Mickey image is on a test pattern on a television screen. Mickey-shaped locks are hanging above the TV in the same window.

Hint 123: Inside the store, a classic Mickey image is formed by the ends of rollers on a mechanical device, which sits to the right of a small fan near the middle of a top shelf along a wall.

- Big Top Toys store

Hint 124: Inside the store, a gray classic Hidden Mickey, tilted to the right, hides on the dapple horse at the lower middle of the mural behind the cashier's counter. The Hidden Mickey is located on the right side of the horse's neck, just above the decorative orange reins.

- near Oswald's

Hint 125: On a wall above and to the right of the Chamber of Commerce building near Oswald's, a blue painted advertisement says "Elias and Company, Open 7 Days." A tiny white classic Mickey hides along the inner border of the blue area, to the right of the "N" in "Open."

- Buena Vista Street Trolley Station

Hint 126: At the trolley station waiting area near the main park entrance, a classic Mickey made of rocks hides in the support pillar nearest the park entrance. It's under the four vertical red bricks, which are at the top of the outer right side of the pillar. This Hidden Mickey is tilted to the left, and the left "ear" has striped markings.

Main Entrance Plaza

Hint 127: Ironwork gratings surround some tree trunks in the entrance plaza. Tiny classic Mickey fasteners hold a few of the ironwork bands in place.

Hint 128: You'll find classic Mickey holes inside the braces that support the plaza's ticket-booth counters.

Paradise Bay

- World of Color

Hint 129: Watch for the *Up* scene on the water screen during the *World of Color* show. After the *Up* house has floated off the screen, a Mickey balloon soars up and sails off in the direction of the house.

Notes

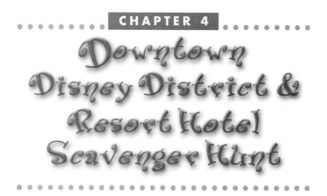

CHAPTER 4

Downtown Disney District & Resort Hotel Scavenger Hunt

Because you may want to hunt only one area at a time, I've listed the perfect score for each area in parentheses after its name in the Clues section.

Downtown Disney District
(58 points)

Begin your Downtown Disney search at the entrance across from the Disneyland Hotel at about 11:00 a.m. to give yourself time to complete this hunt.

Clue 1: Admire paintings along the sidewalk entrance for Hidden Mickeys.
3 points for one or more

Clue 2: Study the Rainforest Cafe outside sign for a Hidden Mickey.
3 points

★ Enter the **D Street** store.

Clue 3: Search a wall inside the store for Mickey on a belt buckle.
4 points

Clue 4: Look around for a red brick Mickey.
3 points

★ Check out the **Disney Vault 28** shop.

Clue 5: Locate a classic Mickey in an upper window of the store.
4 points

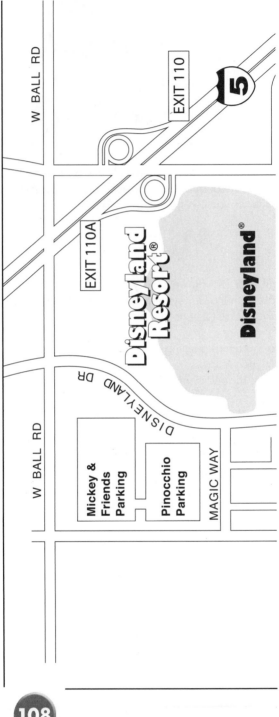

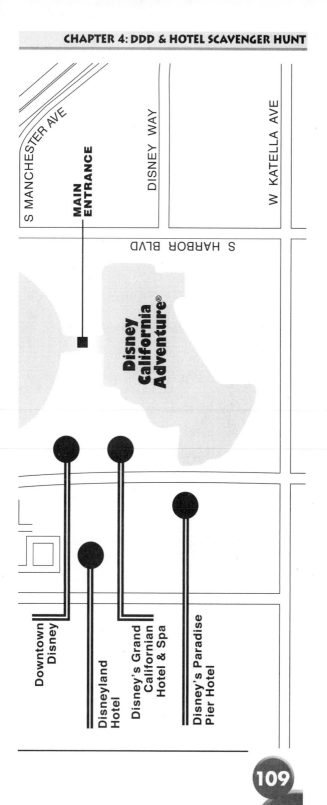

Clue 6: Search for two Mickeys on a wall at the entrance.
5 points for finding both

★ Walk into **Ridemakerz** store.

Clue 7: Locate a classic Mickey on a silver wheel.
5 points

★ Your next stop is **Marceline's Confectionery**.

Clue 8: Find a Hidden Mickey outside the store.
3 points

★ Continue on to **Naples Ristorante e Pizzeria**.

Clue 9: Look up for Mickey outside the restaurant.
3 points

★ Stroll over to the **World of Disney** store nearby.

Clue 10: Find Hidden Mickeys outside the store.
1 point

Clue 11: Search for a classic Mickey on a mural near Lady and the Tramp in the Princess room in the middle of the store.
4 points

Clue 12: Now look for nine classic Mickeys on another mural in the Princess room.
5 points for finding all nine

Clue 13: Locate a classic Mickey on a mural near Cruella De Vil in the Princess room.
4 points

Clue 14: In another room, squint for a Hidden Mickey in a mural with bubbles. (Psst: It's near a washtub.)
4 points

Clue 15: Find Mickey on some merchandise stands.
2 points

Clue 16: Admire the merchandise bins!
3 points for two Hidden Mickeys

Clue 17: Study the kiosks *near the entrance plaza*.
2 points

★ Now head for the *Mickey & Friends Parking Structure* to find more Hidden Mickeys. You can walk there or take a tram from Downtown Disney.

Mickey & Friends Parking Structure
(17 points)

Clue 18: Stop and look up at the directional sign on the *walkway near the tram stop*.
2 points

Clue 19: *Inside the parking structure*, walk up to Level 2 (Daisy Level) and find a Hidden Mickey between poles 3A and 3B.
5 points

Clue 20: Now search near pole 2A.
4 points

Clue 21: While still inside the parking structure, walk to the front of the parking level to spot a Hidden Mickey on a sign. (Psst: It's posted on an entrance car ramp.)
4 points

★ Hop on the *tram to the parks*.

Clue 22: Spot Mickey on a pole.
2 points

★ Make your way back to Downtown Disney, then walk over to *Disney's Grand Californian Hotel & Spa*.

Disney's Grand Californian
Hotel & Spa
(75 points)

★ Look around **outside the main entrance**.

Clue 23: Search for Mickey's full face on a panel.
5 points

Clue 24: In this same area, find classic Mickeys on four different panels.
5 points for four or more

★ Now **enter the lobby**.

Clue 25: Search low for a Hidden Mickey.
3 points

Clue 26: Study the front of the main registration counters for a "conductor Mickey."
5 points

Clue 27: Now search the front of these registration counters nearby for a classic Mickey.
4 points

Clue 28: Finally, search the front of the registration counters one last time for a Hidden Tinker Bell.
5 points

Clue 29: Glance behind the main registration counters for a classic Mickey on a tree.
4 points

Clue 30: Look for two other classic Mickeys behind the main registration counters.
4 points for finding both

Clue 31: Search the other registration counter at the far left (as you face the main registration counter) for three Hidden Mickeys.
5 points for finding all three

Clue 32: This Hidden Mickey knows what time it is!
5 points

Clue 33: Spot a Mickey image on a desk.
3 points

Clue 34: Locate Hidden Mickeys on telephones.
2 points for spotting two or more

Clue 35: Find Mickey on a map.
3 points

Clue 36: Look for Mickey on a wall in the hallway with the restrooms not far from the registration counters.
4 points

Clue 37: Search for Mickey near the fireplace.
3 points

★ Enter the **Hearthstone Lounge**.

Clue 38: Check around for a Hidden Mickey.
2 points

★ If you're hungry, snack inside Hearthstone Lounge or try to get seated for lunch at Storytellers Café.

★ Stroll through the **Downtown Disney exit doors** and turn around.

Clue 39: Look up for a Hidden Mickey.
4 points

Clue 40: Now locate Mickey close to the walkway.
2 points

★ Return to the main lobby and take the **exit that leads to Disney California Adventure** Park.

Clue 41: After a few steps, look up for Mickey.
3 points

★ Head back to the Grand Californian lobby once more and stroll out the front entrance to **Disneyland Drive** (which will take you over to Disney's Paradise Pier Hotel if you are up for more Mickey hunting now).

Clue 42: Find Mickey on a sign.
2 points

Clue 43: Search for Mickey bike racks.
2 points

★ When you are ready to continue your Mickey sleuthing, stroll over to **Disney's Paradise Pier Hotel**.

Disney's Paradise Pier Hotel
(49 points)

Clue 44: Spot Mickey on a wall outside the front entrance of the hotel.
4 points

★ Step **inside the hotel**.

Clue 45: Study a painting in the lobby for a Hidden Mickey.
4 points

Clue 46: Find a telephone nearby for another Hidden Mickey.
2 points

Clue 47: Spot Mickey near the fitness center and the Beachcomber Club.
4 points for finding both

Clue 48: Look inside the elevators for classic Mickeys.
2 points for two or more

Clue 49: Find a Hidden Mickey near the elevators.
2 points

Clue 50: Mickey is near the swimming pool.
2 points

Clue 51: Don't miss Mickey in the Game Room!
2 points

Clue 52: Check out the Vending Room for Hidden Mickeys.
4 points for two Hidden Mickeys

Clue 53: Locate Mickey in a photo in a hallway near the lobby.
5 points

★ Search for classic Mickeys in **Disney's PCH Grill** restaurant.

Clue 54: Study the carpet.
2 points

Clue 55: Search for Mickeys of different sizes in the wall décor.
3 points for finding both sizes

Clue 56: Look for Mickey on lamps.
2 points

Clue 57: Find Mickey in a picture.
1 point

Clue 58: Spot two Mickeys on the ceiling.
2 points for spotting both

Clue 59: Search for three camouflaged Mickeys on three separate surfboards.
5 points for sleuthing out all three

Clue 60: Find two Mickeys on entrance doors.
2 points for spotting both

★ Search **outside the hotel's rear entrance**.

Clue 61: You can't miss Mickey outside the first-floor rear entrance.
1 point

★ Your final stop: the **Disneyland Hotel**.

Disneyland Hotel
(61 points)

★ Check out the area **outside the front entrance**.

Clue 62: Spot Hidden Mickeys in the nearby parking lot.
1 point

Clue 63: While you're at the hotel entrance, don't miss Mickey on the luggage carts.
1 point

★ Step into the **lobby**.

Clue 64: Search for tiny Hidden Mickeys in the registration lobby.
4 points

Clue 65: Study the mirrored glass walls inside the elevators for Mickey.
4 points

★ Take the central lobby elevator down a floor and look around.

Clue 66: Can you spot two Hidden Mickeys, one complete and one partial?
4 points for finding both

★ Return to the main lobby.

Clue 67: Study nearby telephones for Hidden Mickeys.
2 points

★ Now look **around the hotel complex** to find more Hidden Mickeys.

Clue 68: Spot a Hidden Mickey in the Convention Center area.
2 points

Clue 69: Search the floor **near Goofy's Kitchen** for a Hidden Mickey.
5 points

Clue 70: Don't overlook Mickey on the stair handrail!
1 point

Clue 71: Look up for two Mickey images above the top of a staircase.
4 points for both

Clue 72: Upstairs from Goofy's Kitchen, find a painting of Toontown on the wall and study it to spot two Hidden Mickeys.
4 points for finding both

Clue 73: In a painting nearby of a *Splash Mountain* scene, look for three Hidden Mickeys.
5 points for spotting all three

Clue 74: Locate a painting of *Space Mountain*. It has a Hidden Mickey, too!
3 points

Clue 75: Stroll the hotel hallways **near the Sleeping Beauty Pavilion** for Hidden Mickeys at your feet.
2 points for one or more

Clue 76: Look around for two more Mickey images near telephones close to the Sleeping Beauty Pavilion.
4 points for finding both

Clue 77: Near the Sleeping Beauty Pavilion, scrutinize a painting of a jungle temple for a Hidden Mickey.
5 points

★ Walk into the **Frontier Tower lobby**.

Clue 78: Glance around to find Mickey.
2 points

Clue 79: Near the Frontier Tower lobby, locate classic Mickeys on a dress.
4 points

Clue 80: Also near the lobby, look for a painting with two Mickey hats.
4 points for both

Time now to see how you did.

Total Points for Downtown Disney and the Resort Hotels =

How'd You Do?

Up to 104 points - Bronze
105 to 207 points - Silver
208 points and over - Gold
260 points - Perfect Score

Below are the perfect scores for each area in the scavenger hunt, along with the qualifying points for gold (80% of perfect) and bronze (40%). If your score fell somewhere in between the latter two, give yourself silver.

Downtown Disney
Perfect - 58 points; Gold - 46; Bronze - 23

My Score:

Mickey & Friends Parking Structure
Perfect - 17 points; Gold - 14; Bronze - 7

My Score:

Disney's Grand Californian Hotel & Spa
Perfect - 75 points; Gold - 60; Bronze - 30

My Score:

Disney's Paradise Pier Hotel
Perfect - 49 points; Gold - 39; Bronze - 20

My Score:

Disneyland Hotel
Perfect - 61 points; Gold - 49; Bronze – 24

My Score:

**Caution:
Don't peek at this
section unless you
really want help!**

Downtown Disney District

Hint 1: At the entrance to Downtown Disney from Disneyland Hotel, tile paintings created by children are posted along the right side of the walkway across from the ESPN Zone store. Small classic Hidden Mickeys can usually be found in the paintings. (Note: These paintings are changed periodically.)

Hint 2: At the left side of the Rainforest Cafe sign, a classic Hidden Mickey, tilted to the left, is in the middle of the circular bumps on the green lizard's neck.

- D Street

Hint 3: A full-body image of an angry Mickey Mouse is painted on the left back wall of the second room. A black classic Mickey hides on his belt buckle, which is often hidden behind merchandise.

119

Hint 4: A large classic Mickey shaped of faux bricks is located on a recessed wall behind a store register in the third room. This Hidden Mickey is often partially covered by paintings.

- Disney Vault 28

Hint 5: A classic Mickey head hides above crossbones in the window just below the right side of the large "Disney Vault 28" outdoor sign.

Hint 6: A tiny classic Mickey is stuck on the upper right of the large metal vault door that forms the back wall of the entrance vestibule of the store, while an upside-down classic Mickey can be found on the vault door's lower right.

- Ridemakerz

Hint 7: A red, white, and black classic Hidden Mickey (with stylized white "R" and red "Z" letters on the "head" and each "ear" of the Mickey) hides on the back of a silver metal wheel with spokes. Find this wheel perched high atop a display of small model cars at the front of the store and look at the middle of the wheel.

- Marceline's Confectionery

Hint 8: On the sign in front of the store, swirls in the letters "M" and "C" combine to form a classic Mickey.

- Naples Ristorante e Pizzeria

Hint 9: In front of the restaurant, near the top edge of the pizza sign at the "1:00 o'clock" position, three circular pepperonis form a sideways classic Mickey.

- World of Disney

Hint 10: Blue classic Mickeys adorn the corners of the large signs over the entrance doorways to the store.

Hint 11: Go to the Princess room (near the center of the store) and check out the right side of the room near the ceiling for the mural above an opening to the next room. Search the mural for a bridge with a covered walkway. A classic Mickey hides above the center arch of the walkway. The bridge is behind Goofy the Gondolier and Lady and the Tramp sharing spaghetti.

Hint 12: Nine classic Mickeys can be spotted in a mural of the world on the wall behind the service counter in the Princess room. One light brown and six small red classic Mickeys are on the middle and bottom of the mural, and two dark blue classic Mickeys are at the top middle of the mural.

Hint 13: In a mural near the ceiling on the left side of the Princess room, a white classic Mickey hides on an Oriental archway to the right of several Dalmatians.

Hint 14: Murals with bubbles are high on the walls of a room near the end of the store closest to the parks. One mural on the right side of the room has three bubbles that form a small classic Mickey tilted to the left. Find it near the center of the mural, to the right of a white plate that's floating in the air over a brown washtub. The Hidden Mickey is tilted toward the white plate and is almost completely sideways. A bubble bigger than the ears overlaps with the right side of Mickey's "head."

Hint 15: As in many shops on Disney property, classic Mickey holes are in some of the merchandise pole supports.

Hint 16: Some of the round merchandise bins have classic Mickeys encircling the top and classic Mickey-shaped feet.

- Kiosks near the entrance plaza

Hint 17: The eaves of several kiosks sport classic Mickey-shaped supports.

Mickey & Friends Parking Structure

- *Walkway near the tram stop*

Hint 18: On the walkway near the tram stop, a classic Mickey sits atop the sign that points the way to Mickey & Friends Parking Structure.

Hint 19: A classic Mickey is etched in the cement midway between poles 3A and 3B, next to an unnumbered pole and under an "Emergency" sign.

Hint 20: A classic Mickey is etched in the cement two car stalls over from pole 2A, as you head toward the exit drive path.

Hint 21: Look for a yellow sign on a wall at one end of an automobile entrance ramp at the side of the walkway to the Trams. A classic Mickey is at the top of a "Caution – U-Turn" sign.

- *Tram to the parks*

Hint 22: Classic Mickeys top the light poles that line the tram path from the Mickey & Friends Parking Structure to the parks. (You can spot these light pole Mickeys in other areas around the Disneyland Resort property, such as in some of the parking lots.)

Disney's Grand Californian Hotel & Spa

- *Outside the main entrance*

Hint 23: A pillar just outside the main entrance is covered with colorful panels. On the rear panel, a three-quarter image of Mickey's face looks out from between the outer branches of a tree. He's about three-quarters of the way up the left side of the tree.

Hint 24: On this same rear panel, a classic Mickey is at the middle bottom of the tree, just above the trunk.

 In fact, you can spot small classic Mickeys in some of the trees on all four panels around this pillar!

- Lobby area and nearby hallways

Hint 25: As you enter the Grand Californian lobby, look for a rug with the hotel's tree logo to spot the small classic Mickey above the tree's trunk. (Wherever you come across the Grand Californian Hotel logo, you're likely to spot a classic Mickey in the lower middle of the tree branches.)

Hint 26: A small side view of Mickey Mouse is sculpted in tile on the front desk. Toward the middle of the long counter, look for dancing bears on a panel in a depression in the desk. Mickey Mouse is conducting with a wand to the right of the white bear.

Hint 27: To the right of "conductor Mickey" is a brown, raised classic Mickey on the lower middle part of a tree.

Hint 28: To the left of "conductor Mickey" is a figure of Tinker Bell near (and to the immediate left of) a flat, dark writing surface.

Hint 29: On a fabric mural on the far left side of the rear wall behind the main registration counters, a dark classic Mickey hides just above the trunk in the branches of the leftmost tree.

Hint 30: You can spot two classic Mickeys on the left side of a fabric mural that hangs on the far right side of the rear wall behind the main registration counters. One is below the second maroon line from the top and the other is above the fifth maroon line from the top.

Hint 31: On the registration counter to the far left (as you face the main registration counters), look for ceramic green trees on each side of the front of the counter. Classic Mickeys are in their lower branches. A third classic Mickey sits in the lower middle branches of a tiny light-yellow tree to the upper left of the green tree on the right side of the counter.

Hint 32: A classic Mickey depression is on the face of the grandfather clock in the main lobby.

Hint 33: A classic Mickey hole is in the middle front of a desk, high up under the projecting lip of the desktop. The desk is usually at the rear left of the main lobby.

Hint 34: Telephones near the lobby elevators sport two classic Mickeys each, one above a touchtone button at the lower part of the phone information panel and another at the top of the panel in the tree logo for the Grand Californian hotel. You'll also find the tree-logo classic Mickey on the dials of rotary phones near the lobby.

Hint 35: On a map of the Grand Californian on a wall along a walkway at the left (as you enter) of the main lobby, the Children's Pool area is shaped like a classic Mickey.

Hint 36: In the nearby hallway to the left of the main entrance (as you face in from the entrance), classic Mickeys are in the corners of the frame of a painting that hangs on the wall near the restrooms. The painting shows a rocky and mountainous coastline.

Hint 37: A classic Mickey made of round stones and tilted to the right is in the lower front part of the rock wall on the left side of the lobby fireplace.

- Hearthstone Lounge

Hint 38: Classic Mickey holes repeat near the outer rim of some of the large light fixtures hanging from the ceiling in the Hearthstone Lounge.

- Walkway to Downtown Disney

Hint 39: As you start along the walkway to Downtown Disney District, turn around and look up to spot a classic Mickey on the Grand Californian logo tree in an upper-story window.

Hint 40: Classic Mickeys adorn each of the Grand Californian tree logos that are embossed on the planters lining the walkway to Downtown Disney.

- Walkway to Disney California Adventure

Hint 41: The side panels of the lamps along the walkway to the Disney California Adventure Park entrance are embellished with tree designs. The tallest tree on each panel has a classic Mickey in its lower branches.

- Disneyland Drive

Hint 42: The large Grand Californian entrance signs facing Disneyland Drive include the hotel's tree logo with its classic Mickey.

Hint 43: As you face the Grand Californian Hotel from Disneyland Drive, look for a Cast Member entrance driveway to the right of the main entrance to the hotel. Bicycle racks shaped as classic Mickeys are along the left side of this driveway.

Disney's Paradise Pier Hotel

- Outside the front entrance

Hint 44: Classic Mickey impressions are in the gray recessed wall just to the left of the front entrance (as you face the hotel).

- Inside the hotel

Hint 45: A large painting of a stylized Paradise Pier hangs on a wall facing the main entrance. In the painting's upper right, a black classic Mickey tilted to the right hides inside a red cart on a Ferris wheel. (It might be Mickey himself!)

Hint 46: Telephones near the central lobby sport a classic Mickey above one of the touchtone buttons along the bottom.

Hint 47: On the second floor, you'll find classic Mickey wooden cutouts in the trim above the entrances to both Mickey's Beach Workout Room and the Beachcomber Club. (An entrance door to the fitness center also features a large decorative classic-Mickey window.)

Hint 48: Classic Mickeys are scattered in the colorful designs of surfboards on the inside elevator walls.

Hint 49: White classic Mickeys appear in the dark blue guest hallway carpets. (Note: Carpets change from time to time, but you can usually find Hidden Mickeys in any new carpets in the hotels.)

Hint 50: On the third floor, classic Mickeys grace the top railings around the swimming pool.

Hint 51: Large partial classic Mickeys top the palm trees along the wall of the Game Room near the lobby elevators.

Hint 52: Stylized paintings in the Vending Room across from the Game Room harbor Hidden Mickeys. At the middle left of one painting, a classic Mickey tilted to the left is on the side of the DisneyQuest building. On the right side of another painting, a classic Mickey is on the side of a roller coaster's support structure.

Hint 53: On a wall across from the Pacific Ballroom, look for a red classic Mickey reflection is in a framed photo of sunset over the water. You see the sun through pier supports.

- Disney's PCH Grill

Hint 54: A multicolored classic Mickey in swirls is woven into the restaurant's carpet.

Hint 55: Small black classic Mickeys hide on diagonal wires on the wall, while a large, black partial classic Mickey hides higher up on the wall near the kitchen.

Hint 56: Black classic Mickeys are on the food lamps hanging in the kitchen area.

Hint 57: A large classic Mickey with the earth as Mickey's head hides in a picture on the wall.

Hint 58: Large black classic Mickeys are near the ceiling in the rear room, one on a red kite and the other on a yellow kite.

Hint 59: Three different surfboards decorating the restaurant's walls shelter classic Mickeys, one in fireworks, one in flowers, and one in black circles at the bottom of the surfboard.

Hint 60: Black partial classic Mickeys hide in the glass panels of each of the double doors at the PHC Grill's entrance.

- Outside the rear entrance

Hint 61: Classic Mickeys are atop short poles just outside the rear entrance to the hotel.

Disneyland Hotel

- Lobby and entrance areas

Hint 62: Classic Mickeys top the light poles in the main entrance parking lot.

Hint 63: Classic Mickeys are hiding in the middle of the side railings of the luggage carts.

Hint 64: In the lobby, several blue rectangular panels decorate the front of the long registration counter. These panels contain many tiny bubbles of different sizes that form classic Mickeys at intervals.

Hint 65: On the mirrored glass on the left side wall of the elevators (as you face the doors from inside), a small white classic Mickey hides in the stars near the elevator doors.

Hint 66: Below the central lobby, look for the room where "Lost and Found" is located. A complete classic Mickey is formed by the silver push panels on a set of swinging doors, while a partial Mickey is on the push panel of the single door marked, "Cast Members Only."

Hint 67: Back upstairs, each of the telephones in the hallways near the central lobby sports a classic Mickey above one of the touchtone buttons at the bottom.

- Around the hotel complex

Hint 68: Inside the hotel, in the Convention Center area to the right, you can usually find classic Hidden Mickeys in the carpet.

Hint 69: To the right of Goofy's Kitchen and Steakhouse 55, umbrellas hanging from the ceiling sport classic Hidden Mickeys.

Hint 70: Gold classic Mickeys are atop the ends of the middle handrail on the stairs near Goofy's Kitchen.

Hint 71: On the ceiling at the top of a staircase near Goofy's Kitchen, a large classic Mickey on a blue background is secured by small classic Mickey bolts.

Hint 72: Find the woman wearing a red dress in the right lower section of a stylized painting of Toontown. The two children with her are wearing Mickey ears.

Hint 73: Look at the lower right section of the painting of a scene in front of *Splash Mountain*. From left to right, you can spot three classic Mickeys: a red Mickey balloon, a small white and black Mickey balloon, and, at the far right of the painting, a child with Mickey ears.

Hint 74: Glance around for a painting of *Space Mountain*. In the sky at the upper left is a fireworks classic Mickey tilted to the left.

- Near Sleeping Beauty Pavilion

Hint 75: Classic Mickeys are in the carpet in the hallways near the Sleeping Beauty Pavilion and the Magic Kingdom Ballroom.

Hint 76: On the bank of telephones near the hallway adjacent to the Sleeping Beauty Pavilion, classic Mickeys are on the light covers and Mickey silhouettes are on the dividers between the phones.

Hint 77: Across from the Sleeping Beauty Pavilion, a classic Mickey hides in a painting of a jungle temple. It's on the top front of the hood of a jeep at the lower middle of the painting.

- Frontier Tower Lobby

Hint 78: In the Frontier Tower Lobby, ottomans are often arranged in a classic Mickey formation. You'll often find the same arrangement in the Fantasy and Adventure Towers.

Hint 79: In a hallway to the left of the lobby, check out the right wall next to the stairwell for a painting of a steamboat landing. In its foreground, a woman walks with two children. Her dress has a classic Mickey pattern.

Hint 80: In the stairwell itself (leading down from the hallway to the left of the Frontier Tower lobby), look for a painting with the word "Frontierland." A child in a train car in the middle of the painting is wearing Mickey ears, as is a man in the stagecoach at the top of the painting.

Other Mickey Appearances

These Hidden Mickeys won't earn you any points, but you're bound to enjoy them if you're in the right place at the right time to see them.

Look for holiday Hidden Mickeys if you're at Disneyland during the Christmas season, or for that matter, any major holiday.

Other "Hidden" Mickeys – décor and deliberate – appear with some regularity throughout the Disneyland Resort. Notice the Mickster on Disneyland brochures, maps and flags, Cast Member name tags, Cast Member uniforms, guest room keys, pay telephones and phone books, and restaurant and store receipts. The restaurants sometimes offer classic Mickey butter and margarine pats, pancakes and waffles, and pizzas and pasta, as well as Mickey napkins. They also arrange dishes and condiments to form classic Mickeys. Some condiment containers are even shaped like Mickey. You might notice classic Mickey holes in the backs of some high chairs. Road signs on Disneyland property may sport Mickey ears, and Disneyland vehicles and monorails may display Mickey Mouse insignia.

Cleaning personnel will often spray the ground, windows, furniture, and other items with three circles of cleaning solution (a classic Mickey) before the final cleansing. Or they may leave three wet Mickey Mouse circles or other Disney character images on the pavement after mopping! Mickey even decorates manhole covers, survey markers, and utility covers in the ground, as you've probably already discovered for yourself.

Enjoy all these Mickeys as you enjoy Disneyland. And if you want to take some home with you, rest assured that you can always find "Hidden" Mickeys on souvenir mugs, merchandise bags and boxes, T-shirts, and Christmas tree ornaments sold in the Disneyland shops. So even when you're far away from Disneyland, you can continue to enjoy Hidden Mickeys.

To enjoy a Hidden Mickey from above, check out Google Earth and find the classic Mickey created by two sidewalks on either side of Disneyland Drive approaching Katella Avenue—below and just to the right of Disney's Paradise Pier Hotel in the Google Earth image. The sidewalks form a distorted image, but the voters on my website liked it as a Hidden Mickey. I hope you will, too.

To access the image, go to Google Earth (download the program from GoogleEarth.com), type in "Disneyland, California," and click on the "Search" button next to the destination. Then scroll with your mouse to the left and down until you're just below the Paradise Pier hotel, and you'll see the palm-outlined Hidden Mickey. (The palm-lined sidewalks form the head and ears). You may have to play around with the dials at the upper right of the window to get a good view. (Note: The trees are covering up the image more and more in recent years.)

My Favorite Hidden Mickeys

• •

In this field guide, I've described more than 480 Hidden Mickeys at the Disneyland Resort. I enjoy every one of them, but the following are extra special to me. They're special because of their uniqueness, their deep camouflage (which makes them especially hard to find), or the "Eureka!" response they elicit when I spot them—or any combination of the above. Here then are my Favorite Hidden Mickeys at Disneyland. I apologize to you if your favorite Hidden Mickey is not (yet) on the list below.

My Top Ten

1. Conductor Mickey. Check the registration counter at Disney's Grand Californian Hotel & Spa and marvel at this magnificent (but tiny) rendition of Mickey conducting an imagined musical symphony for the dancing bears nearby. You'll feel like singing along! (Clue 26, Chap. 4)

2. Randall's Mickey. In the *Monster's Inc.* ride, Hollywood Land, Disney California Adventure Park, the little girl Boo pounds monster Randall with a bat. As Randall (who looks like a lizard and changes color like a chameleon) changes colors, a classic Mickey sometimes appears on his belly. This great Mickey image is intermittent, so stare long and hard at poor Randall, and don't wince! (Clue 36, Chap. 3)

3. Mountain Snow Mickey, Disneyland Park. There's more than snow on the Disneyland Matterhorn! Admire the majestic mountain from near *"it's a small world"* for a Mickey clearing in the snow. (Clue 9, Chap. 2)

4. Mr. Toad's Door Mickey, Fantasyland, Disneyland Park. You mustn't miss this marvelous Mickey image on the right door (lower left corner) of the third set of doors you crash through at the beginning of *Mr. Toad's Wild Ride*. Try not to wreck your car looking for it! (Clue 26, Chap. 2)

5. Mickey Smiling Out From A Tree. Out front of Disney's Grand Californian Hotel & Spa, observe a three-quarter view of Mickey's face peering out from between the branches of a tree on a ceramic panel on one of the columns. Yes, he's smiling at you! (Clue 23, Chap. 4)

6. Pirate-Armor Mickey, Adventureland, Disneyland. It must've been one proud pirate who wore this Mickey armor breastplate which you'll find on *Pirates of the Caribbean*. I feel a song coming on: "Yo, ho, yo, ho, a pirate's life for me." (Clue 36, Chap. 2)

7. Purple Car-Hood Mickey. This faint white classic Mickey on a car hood inside Ramone's House of Body Art in Cars Land, Disney California Adventure, is a clever touch by the artist. You may need help from a Cast Member to find it! (Clue 103, Chap. 3)

8. Winnie the Pooh's Tree Mickey. As you take off in your beehive in *The Many Adventures of Winnie the Pooh*, Critter Country, Disneyland Park, squint to your right to admire this subtle classic Mickey in the bark of a tree. When you see it, you'll want to bounce like Tigger! (Clue 101, Chap. 2)

9. Big Ben Mickey. A side view of Mickey's face is below you in a window of Big Ben during *Peter Pan's Flight* in Disneyland's Fantasyland. Look back to spot Mickey in London! (Clue 7, Chap. 2)

10. Mark Twain Mickey. Make a special trip to Frontierland, Disneyland Park, to find Mickey on a steamboat. He's standing by two well-dressed women on the lower deck of the *Mark Twain Riverboat*. Mickey in a tux! (Clue 59, Chap. 2)

Ten Honorable Mentions

1. Sunset Mickey. Journey to Disney's Paradise Pier Hotel to gawk at the sunset classic Mickey in the photo on the wall near the Pacific Ballroom. How did they do that? (Clue 53, Chap. 4)

2. Nemo Rock Mickey. Make a special effort to chase down this classic Mickey in a rock wall in Tomorrowland, Disneyland Park, near both the elevator for the *Disneyland Monorail* and *Finding Nemo Submarine Voyage*. You won't regret it! (Clue 65, Chap. 2)

3. Pinocchio Ship Mickey. Pinocchio is a classic, and so is this hard-to-spot, elegant classic Mickey on a model ship's case in *Pinocchio's Daring Journey*, Fantasyland, Disneyland. Ahoy, Mickey! (Clue 119, Chap. 2)

4. Clock Mickey. A subtle classic Mickey impression adorns the face of the grandfather clock in the lobby of Disney's Grand Californian Hotel & Spa. You'll be impressed! (Clue 32, Chap. 4)

5. Spotlight Mickey. Inside *The Twilight Zone Tower of Terror* in Disney California Adventure's Hollywood Land, veer to the left lower elevator loading area to stand under this Mickey in lights. Look up and be amazed! (Clue 79, Chap. 3)

6. Lava Mickey. Along the *Toy Story Midway Mania!* ride, Paradise Pier, Disney California Adventure, don't overlook Mickey in the lava behind a middle-level balloon. You have to pop the balloon to see Mickey. (Clue 8, Chap. 3)

7. Toontown Dalmatian Mickey. Press the doorbell at the Fire Department in Mickey's Toontown in Disneyland, and backpedal to spot a cool Hidden Mickey on the Dalmatian—where else but in the spots! (Clue 147, Chap. 2)

8. Radiator Springs Racers' Electrical Mickey, Cars Land, Disney California Adventure. As you motor along, be quick for this Hidden Mickey on an electrical box in Ramone's Body Art shop. Don't worry, if you meet Luigi instead, you can admire Hidden Mickeys behind Luigi and on a red toolbox to your right. (Clue 3, Chap. 3)

9. Schmoozies Minnie. We can't forget Minnie Mouse! At Schmoozies in Disney California Adventure's Hollywood Land, Minnie looks positively regal as the Statue of Liberty. (Clue 60, Chap. 3)

10. Ridemakerz Mickey. This colorful Hidden Mickey is inside the Ridemakerz store in Downtown Disney District. Don't be surprised—it's on a silver racecar wheel! (Clue 7, Chap. 4)

Don't Stop Now! . . . .

Hidden Mickey mania is contagious. The benign pastime of searching out Hidden Mickeys has escalated into a bona fide vacation mission for many Disneyland fans. I'm happy to add my name to the list of hunters. Searching for images of the Main Mouse can enhance a solo trip to the parks or a vacation for the entire family. Little ones delight in spotting and greeting Mickey Mouse characters in the parks and restaurants. As children grow, the Hidden Mickey game is a natural evolution of their fondness for the Mouse.

Join the search! With alert eyes and mind, you can spot Hidden Mickey classics and new ones waiting to be found. Even beginners have happened upon a new, unreported Hidden Mickey or two. As new attractions open and older ones get refurbished, new Hidden Mickeys await discovery.

The Disney entertainment phenomenon is unique in many ways, and Hidden Mickey mania is one manifestation of Disney's universal appeal. Join in the fun! Maybe I'll see you at Disneyland, marveling (like me) at the Hidden Gems. They're waiting patiently for you to discover them.

Acknowledgements. . . . . . .

No Hidden Mickey hunter works alone. While I've spotted most of the Hidden Mickeys in this book on my own — and personally verified every single one of them — finding Hidden Mickeys is an ongoing group effort. I am indebted to the following dedicated Hidden Mickey explorers for alerting me to a number of Hidden Mickeys I might otherwise have missed. Thanks to each and every one of you for putting me on the track of one or more of these Disneyland treasures and, in some cases, also helping me verify them.

Those named in bold letters have spotted 10 or more, which includes current as well as lost Hidden Mickeys. You can find each person's contribution(s) by visiting my website, www.HiddenMickeyGuy.com.

Extra special thanks to Rosemary and Neil (FindingMickey.com) for spotting and helping me verify over 200 Hidden Mickeys at Disneyland **and to Sharon Dale and Sharon Gee** for finding over 50.

Karlos Aguilera, Jonathan Agurcia, Kala'i Ahlo-Souza, The Alberti's, David Almanza, Antonio Altamirano, Bob Anderson, Katrina Andrews, Issac Aragon, Vahe Arevshatian, Cheryl Armstrong, John Axtell, Kristi B., **Brian Babcock**, Kim Bacon and Family, Duane Baker, Jennifer Baker, Ruby Beatrice Baker, Hans Balders, Matt and Shelly and Keira Barbieri, Andrew Bardsley, Katharine and Ammon Barney, Melissa Barrett, Melisa Beardslee, Bradly Behmer, April Beisser, John Benavidez II, Daniel and Elise Berdin, **Brian Bergstrom**, Jenny Bigpond, **Murray Bishop**, Tina Blaylock, Tim Bonanno, Cam Bondoc, Jacob Steven Bonillas, Corey Borgen, Lynn Boyd, Lori Brackett, Chad Bradbury, Erik Bratlien, Vicky Braun, David Breede, Carol Brown, Kaden Brown, Keller Brown, Nicolas Brown, Peter Brown, Thierry and Gabriella and Matthieu Bruxelle, Colin Buchanan, Michael Buell, Josh Burch, Marjorie Burns, Felix Bustos, Nate Buteyn, Amy C., Peter C., Ashley Cabrera, Chris Caflisch, Bev Cain, Stacy Campbell, Craig Canady, Marisa Cardenas, Nicholas Noah Carreno,

Peter Cefalu, Gail Chambers, Leonard Chan, Austin Chanu, Danielle Chard, Chelsi Chipps, Emmy Christopherson, Diana Cimadamore, John Clover, Mary Jo Collins, Jeffrey Colwell, Catherine Conroy, Megan Cook, Michelle Cornelius, **Sherrie Cotton**, Marissa Covarrubias, **Josh and Cassi Cox**, The Coylar Family, Michael Cross, **Sharon Dale**, Erika Davila, Carlos A. de Alba, Jessica de la Vara, Jess Delgado, Jeremiah Dempsey, Jacob DePriest, Tim Devine, Matt Dickerson, Casey Dietz, Thea Dodge, Phillip Donnelly, Tom Donnelly, Jaime Doyle, Maria Dufault, Madison Dunn, Lindsey E., Michael Early, Kyle Edison, Chad Elliot, John Emmert, Scott Evans, Miranda Michelle Felice, Joel Feria, Jennifer Fernandez, Troy and Cheyanne Field, Rob Fitzpatrick, Nicholas Fleming, Joe Flowers, Melissa Forte, Keitaro Francisco, Matthew Furstenfeld, Ben G., Curt Gale, **Jason Gall**, Michele Galvez, Jon Gambill, Joshua Garces, Valerie Garren, **Sharon Gee**, Sam Gennawey, Amy Gervais, Staci Gleed, Tyler Glynn, Alec Goldberg, Jimmy Golden, Micheline Golden, Reyna Gonzalez, Jeremiah Good, Jordan Goodman, Alex Goslar, Tim Grassey, Michael Greening, Christine Griffith, Josh Grothem, Kimberly Gryte, Carl H., Dave H., Elaine H., Josh and Alyssa and Melody Hadeen, Michael Hadlock, Holly Haider, John Hall, Sarah Hall, The Hallak Family, Rachel Hammond, Brian Hancock, Jon Handler, Chris Hansen, Cynthia Hess, Kate Heylman, **Mari Highleyman**, Carl Hoffman, Paul Hoffman, **Milton Holecek**, Michael Hollingsworth, Ethan Holmes, Chas Howell, Cory Hughes, Robert Huntington, Malaine Ivy-Decker, Tara Jacob, Molly Jane, Sharise Jaso, Loren Javier, **Mike Johansen**, James Johnson, Amy Jones, Michelle June, Gordon K., Matt K., Tom K., Summer Kane, Jennifer Kanihan, Andranik Karapetian, **Mehlanie Kayra**, Ryan Kehoe, Della Kingsland, Xela Knarf, Andrew Knight, Matthew and Missy Knoll, Dalia Kuarez, Meghan Kueny-Thornburg, Chase L., Christine Lamar, Kimberly Lamb, Rhonda Lampitt, Ledawn Larsen, Cortney Laurence, Martin Lee, Phillip Lemon, Andrew Lepire, Tony Lepore, Annie Lin, Ronald Lindberg, Alysia Lippetti, Myrna Litt, Ryan Lizama, Lourdes Llanes, Allison Lloyd, Joe Loecsey, Amber Lopez, Brian Z. Lucas, Katherine Lugo, Sal Lugo, Thao Luong, Austin M., Christina M., Henry Macall, Heather Mackey, Hank Mahler,

Maria Maki, C. Mallonee, Cori Mallonee, Jorge Mario, Jasmine Martinez, John Martinez, Juan M. Martinez III, Paul Martinez, Dave Marx, **Michael Mason**, Kim McClaughry, Krystle McClung, Ciara McGovern, James Mcguine, Cindy McKeown, Connor McKeown, Sylvia McNeil, Oscar Mejorada, The Miles Family, Dallas Millam, Randi Miller, Robert Miller, Amanda Mitton, Kotomi Miyajima, Sandy Montelongo, Christopher Morales, Jose Moran, Carlos Moreno, Rebecca Mortin, Danny Mui, The Muklewicz Family, Tom Nadzieja, Lindsey Naizer, **Bobby Naus**, Kristen Naus, Andy Neitzert, A. Nelson, Aly Nelson, Aryn Nelson, Marina Nelson, Dave and Kim Ness, Jay Nicholson, Ty Nielson, Daniel Nieto, Joseph Nolan, Jen O'Bryan, Elaine Ojeda, Michael and Wendy Olayvar, Jennifer Oliphant, Orlando Attractions magazine, **Steve Orme**, Greg Ostravich, Jessica Outhet, Andrew P., Joey P., Monica Garcia Montero P., Sam P., Priscilla Padilla, Shawna Park, Steve Parmley, Justin Parnell, Cherna Patterson, Mark Pellegrini, Cheyenne Pemberton, Rob and Buffy and Anna and Julia Penttila, Jennifer Peterson, Christopher Phelan, Leslie Phillips, Eric Polk, Roger Pollard, Diana Poncini, Heather Pone, Robert Powers, Kaitlyn Pratt, Melanie Price, Alyssa Proudfoot, Carlos Quintanilla, Marv R., Louise Rafferty, BJ Ralphs, Angel Ramirez, Sal Ramirez, Brendan Ratner, Sara Reid, Caleb Richards, Linda Richards, Marv Richards, Joy E. Robertson-Finley, Jeff Robinson, Jose Rodriguez, Katie Rogers, Geoff Rogos, George Rojas, Shaun Rosen, Todd Rosspencer, Jean Rowley, Julian Rucki, Jessica Ruggles, Caleb Ruiz, Richard Ruiz, **Russ Rylee**, John Salinas, Jennifer Salvatierra, Dominic Sanna, Bianca and Nathan and Isaac Santaro, Brandie Sargent, Candace and Emily and Ethan Sauter, Andy Schelb, Kaleigh Schiro, Zod Schultz, P. Schwarz, Chris Scott, Kira Scott, Tim Scott, Lauren Seibert, Khrys Sganga, Nate Sharp, Michael Shearin, Mark Sheppard, The Sherrick Family, Derek Shimozaki, Ryan Shimozaki, Heather Sievers, Zach Simes, Amy Simpson, Shannan Sinclair, Breana Nicole Smith, Rebecca Smith, Jose Solano, Christopher Solesbee, Braden Stanley, Brad Steinbrenner, Lloyd Stevens, Anastasia Stewart, Darrell St. Pierre, Taylor Stratton, Chris Strodder (author of "The Disneyland Book of Lists"), Jessica Strom, Tyler Struck, Rich Sylvester, Erin T., Mitch T., Stacy T., Donna Taing, Stacy Tanaka, Pat Tee,

Nikolas Tejeda, Mark Temte, Craig R. Thompson, Darin Thompson, Sheryl Thompson, Joseph Thorne, Sandy Thornton, Andrew Thorp, The Tierney Family, Tim Titus, Micaela Tracy, Mark Treiger, Eric Upah, Christian Urcia, **Luis Valdez**, Ryan Valle, Kim Vander Dussen, Sam Vanderspek, Jeff Van Ry, Aldo Velez, Evelyn Vides, Juliet Violette, Fred Vosecky, Heather W., Ron W., Brock Waidmann, Mel Waidmann III, Melvin Waidmann II, Rhonda Waidmann, William Waidmann, Barrie and Jack Waldman-Marker, Scott and Kate Walker, Matt Walsh, Yvonne Washburn, Austin Weber, Angela Welliver, Carolyn Whiteford, Christopher Williams, Deb Wills, Ken Wilson, Emily Woods, Gracie Wright, Laura Wright, Jeanine Yamanaka, Lynn Yaw, Ava Z., and Monique Zimmer.

AND

AJ, Alan, Alex, Alexa, Alexz, Amanda, Amber, Amy, Angel, Ari, Audrey, Austin, BP, Brittany, Burley, Cathy, Celandra, Cherna, Chris, Christopher, C.J., C.K., Claire, Cole, Cori, Danny, Dee, Derrick, Destiny, Elizabeth, Emily, Eric, **Eric and Colleen and Julie**, ES, Evan, Hans, Hayden, Hayley, Heather, **Helen and Danny**, Imp, Informer, JC, Jen, Jessica, Jonathan, Josh, Julie, Justin, Kayleigh, Kelsey, Kendra, Kevin, Kim, Krister, KS and CK, Laura, Laura and Lily, Laura and Memoree, Lea Ann, Lloyd, LMD Hidden Mickey Finders, Lori, Luke, Mari, Mark, Matt, Matt@OrlandoAttractionsMagazine, Matthew, Meg, Megan, Melissa, Michaela, Mike, M.L., Morgan, Nathan, Nicky, Nitza, Nix, Nolan, Nusy, Olivia, Peter, Pinky, Queenkoalaandme, Rachel, RaeLynn, Rhonda, **Rosemary and Neil (FindingMickey.com)**, Ryan, Sam, Sandy, Sara, Sarah, Sawyer, Scott, Seeing, Serena, Shannon, Shaun, Shirlyn, Stephanie, Sylvia, **Tamera**, Taylor, Teressa, Tia, Toneto and Laura and Steph, Tracy, Ty, **Where's Mickey (myspace.com/wheresmickey)**, Xander, Ylimegirl, Zod, and Zoe.

Index to Mickey's Hiding Places

● ●

Note: This Index includes only those rides, restaurants, shops, hotels and other places in the Disneyland Resort that harbor confirmed Hidden Mickeys. If the attraction you're looking for isn't included, Mickey isn't hiding there. Or if he is, I haven't yet spotted him.

— *Steve Barrett*

The following abbreviations appear in this Index:

DL – Disneyland Park
CA – Disney California Adventure Park
DD – Downtown Disney District
RH – Resort Hotel